THE DOG LOVER'S GUIDE TO DATING

Using Cold Noses to Find Warm Hearts

BY DEBORAH WOOD

HOWELL
BOOK
HOUSE

Howell Book House

Published by Wiley Publishing, Inc., Indianapolis, IN

For general information on our other products and services or to obtain technical support please contact our Customer Care Department within the U.S. at 800-762-2974, outside the U.S. at 317-572-3993 or fax 317-572-4002.

Wiley also publishes its books in a variety of electronic formats. Some content that appears in print may not be available in electronic books.

Library of Congress Cataloging-in-Publication Data:

Wood, Deborah, date.
  The dog lover's guide to dating : using cold noses to find warm hearts
/ by Deborah Wood.
     p. cm.
  ISBN 0-7645-2501-8 (alk. paper)
  1. Dating (Social customs) 2. Man-woman relationships. 3.
Human-animal relationships. 4. Human-animal communication. 5.
Dogs—Behavior. 6. Dogs—Training. I. Title: Guide to dating : using
cold noses to find warm hearts. II. Title.
  HQ801.W83 2003
  646.7'7—dc21
                                         2003008091

10 9 8 7 6 5 4 3 2

All photos copyright © Carole Archer/Archer Photography

Book production by Wiley Publishing, Inc. Composition Services

Also by Deborah Wood from Howell Book House

Top Dogs: Making It to Westminster

Help for Your Shy Dog: Turning Your Terrified Dog Into a Terrific Pet

Contents

Acknowledgments

I can't imagine writing without a lot of help from my friends. I owe a huge debt to the following people, who gave me ideas, told me their stories, made me laugh, and kept telling me to keep writing. Special thanks to Dr. Joel Gavriele-Gold, who shared a lot of time and wisdom for this book. Other people who helped enormously were Joan Harrigan, Andrea Arden, Janine Adams, Shannon Wilkerson, Leah Atwood, Markie Burkhart, Kathy Taylor, Jerry Taylor, Robin Thompson, Elizabeth Knight, Mark Andres, Dr. Mary Lee Nitschke, Michelle Wood, Kerrin Winter-Churchill, Ellie Wyckoff, Jill Miller, Frank Wood, Christine Turner, Phyllis Nistad, Valerie Stern, Dale DeRoest, Patie Ventre, Nikki Moustaki, Jill Critchfield, Matthew Wood, Dr. Sophia Yin, Jean Owen, Maggie Cullen, Karen Kraus, Barbara Baugnon, Mike Miller, Irene Shang, Eileen Doyle, Paula Ratoza, Cheryl Dondino, Luke Bates, Dr. Adrianne Becker, Stacy and Bill Conroy, Angela and Jack Moore, Tracy Thomas, Chris Thomas, Dan Miller, Matt Fitcher, Jay Multanen, Cindi Pruitt, Debbie Sikes,

Acknowledgments

Mitchel Remsing, and Margie Vincent-Roberts. I've been told that a writing life is a lonely life. That certainly hasn't been my experience!

Thanks to the many couples who shared their stories of true love.

Many of the dog tricks in this book come from the Games and Tricks class that Pogo and I took with Susan Fletcher. Thank you Susan for a great class — we're having fun with the tricks!

Carole Archer's terrific photography made this book better than mere words could ever accomplish.

Thanks to Beth Adelman at Howell Book House for keeping me (relatively) calm as the book kept morphing into new things — and for being a helpful and kind editor.

As always, thanks to my muses: Goldie, Radar, Pogo (my Papillons) and Mews the cat. You make every day a joy, my friends.

Chapter 1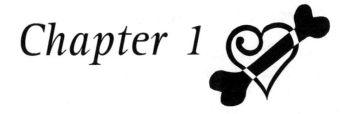

The New Relationship Guru

Looking for a relationship guru is nothing new.

There was the guy who told us that men are from Mars and women are from Venus. All that did for me was reinforce my certain belief that my last lover probably was an extraterrestrial.

There have been a host of writers who've written goofy books about how women are supposed to greet their lovers dressed only in plastic wrap, or how they should follow the Rules and always let the man make every decision. These brief forays back to the 1950s were amusing, but no one I know actually found happiness there (in the decade or in the goofy books).

And what about the workout instructors who were supposed to whip us into shape and make our bodies irresistible? Well, Americans are plumper than ever, and probably some of those plump people used to be aerobics instructors.

No, we've turned to the wrong people to guide us to love. The Venus/Mars relationship guru is as passé as disco dancing. The personal trainer is as obsolete as "getting jiggy with it."

The person of the hour—the individual with the answers to the future happiness of the masses looking for love—is the dog trainer.

Wipe the picture of the old-fashioned dog trainer out of your mind! We're not talking about the guy with the choke collars who made the dogs and people in class behave with military precision. No, your guide to finding love is the modern dog trainer.

More likely than not, today's dog trainer is a slightly overweight woman with a clicker in her hand and permanently encrusted dog treats in the pockets of her baggy jeans. But she can look at an untrained Rottweiler without fear and turn that dog into date bait. Because of her power, a dog trainer is more than a relationship guru; she is a relationship goddess.

I am one of those goddesses. I can teach your dog to attract more people than ever before and to literally fetch a mate for you. I know the best places to go to meet dog lovers, and what you should say to both humans and canines to make them look at you with longing in their eyes.

I know where the bones are buried, so to speak. It's time to unleash your love life.

Chapter 2

Looking for Love in All the Dog Places

The traditional methods of meeting a potential love interest just don't work very well.

Meet someone at a bar? I'm more likely to orchestrate an intervention than ask for the guy's phone number.

Find romance at work? Can you spell *sexual harassment lawsuit?*

You can't be seriously looking for love at the grocery store. Come on! If you see someone suggestively caressing the melons, your first thought isn't, "Now *that's* a normal, functioning adult."

One book I read suggested that singles hang out at banks, since employed people go there to make deposits. But it seems the employed person you'd meet would likely be a police officer or FBI agent during what could be a rigorous and ugly interrogation.

*You're three times more likely to have someone stop and talk to
you if you have a dog with you. I like those odds!*

Probably the worst idea in the history of humankind was the '90s
fad of looking for love at the gym. Let's face it: Some of us are built
more like Pugs than Greyhounds, and trust me when I say that no one
wants to see a Pug in Lycra.

Happily, the answer to the problem is probably lying at your feet
right now. Yes, once again, you'll find that a dog really is man's (and
woman's) best friend.

Your dog is ideal date bait.

Scientific studies have proven it: You're three times more likely to
have someone stop and talk if you have a dog with you.
Psychologists tell us that people with dogs are perceived as friendlier,
more approachable and just plain nicer than those without canine
accomplices.

This book is your guide to the world of meeting, greeting and
falling in love with dog-lovers and their dogs.

Dogs as Date Bait: Why It Works

If you're a dog owner, you know the drill: Walk someplace alone and you're ignored. Walk the same route with your pooch by your side and people will stop and talk.

And they aren't just talking to the dog—they're making eye contact and talking to you. If you play your cards right, your pooch really can lead you to smooch.

There are several reasons why this happens:

 Humans are hardwired to love puppies. We find baby mammals of almost all kinds appealing—and puppies fill the bill in spades. Baby mammals have round heads, large eyes and soft features, and we're biologically driven to look at them, touch them and care for them, just as we are a human baby.

"Infantile features have such a strong effect on us that just looking at a pup can change the balance of hormones in your body," writes Patricia McConnell Ph.D., a dog behaviorist and ethologist (a person who studies animal behavior as the interaction of evolution, genetics, learning and environment) in her book *The Other End of the Leash: Why We Do What We Do Around Dogs.*

Believe it or not, experts call this reaction the "Ahh Factor." It's named that because people see these little creatures and can't help but say "Ahh. . . . "

Some breeds have the soft, sweet looks of puppies even as adults: from Chihuahuas to Cocker Spaniels to Saint Bernards, we've bred dogs that retain the round head, large, luminous eyes and curvy body of a puppy throughout their lives. And we respond with our hormones.

When people stop to pet your puppy—or your puppy-like adult dog—they experience a feeling of maternal or paternal instinct and softness that carries all the way to the human who's with the dog.

Dogs give us permission to talk. "It's like when people wear a T-shirt that says something funny—they're inviting people to look at them," says clinical psychologist Dr. Joel Gavriele-Gold, author of *When Pets Come Between Partners.*

But walking your dog does something more for you than any T-shirt could. While a funny phrase on a shirt might make people laugh, it's just a shirt. You and your dog are a pair, a team. "It gives the message that you're capable of some kind of caring and nurturing," says Gavriele-Gold.

Of course, it doesn't work to buy a dog just to impress potential dates. Most of what makes us attractive is the loving, nurturing, caring relationship we have with our pets, and you can't fake that.

 Dogs allow us into intimate space. Although our personal space requirements vary by culture, all human societies have very clear (although unspoken) rules about how close you can be to another person without being rude.

For example, in the United States anyone who comes within eight to 12 inches of your body is in your "highly personal" space. This space is seldom entered in public, and is usually reserved for our lovers, children and close family. Twelve to 36 inches is the space we usually reserve for good friends, and most business transactions and social conversations take place four and a half to five *feet* away.

Think what happens when you walk your dog. When people stop to pet your dog, they are often only inches away and may even touch you. They've waltzed right into your personal space. Your body is already treating this person as a close friend.

I used to live in a condominium along the riverfront of downtown Portland, Oregon. It's an area that has lots of restaurants, small shops and upscale bars—a popular first-date place. When I'd take my little six-pound Papillon out for walks, it was easy to spot people who were on their first date and liking each other—but not quite ready to touch.

"Can we pet your dog?" they'd ask.

"Sure," I'd say.

I'd hold little Goldie in my arms—and the couple would pet, and pet and pet. They couldn't quite be intimate with one another, but they could use my Goldie as a substitute for touching each other.

"I LOVE dogs," one would invariably say. There—he'd said the word "love" in a safe way in front of the new date.

"It feels so good to TOUCH her," the other would whisper. The woman was giving her date the cue that she really likes to be touched. This date is going well.

While I lived in that condo, this scene was played out hundreds of times. Goldie allowed the couples the first foray into a shared, intimate space.

 Maybe some of it's just plain magic. One study followed a woman walking a Labrador Retriever. Three times as many people stopped and talked with her when she was walking her dog than when she was alone.

Several studies have documented the ability of a dog to break social barriers. These studies followed children who were disfigured by accident or disease. When the children were accompanied by a dog, everything changed. Instead of being isolated, people of all ages stopped and talked with the children.

"People focus on the dog instead of on the person," says Dr. Mary Lee Nitschke, an animal behaviorist and psychology professor at Linfield College. "It's usually threatening to talk to a person in a wheelchair, or any stranger. The dog makes the person seem less threatening."

Whether you've got a serious disability or just feel a little insecure, your dog will break down the barriers you could never crack on your own.

 We have literally evolved together. The magic of our relationship with dogs is lost in the mists of our earliest history.

Luke and Adrianne: A True Love Story

Palmer the Weimaraner didn't look that sick. But he was lethargic, and that wasn't normal for this Weimaraner, who usually had springs on his toes. Luke Bates decided to take his dog to the vet, just in case.

The problem was, he'd just moved to Portland, Oregon, a few weeks before, and he didn't have a veterinarian. He talked with several friends, and they all recommended the Laurelhurst Veterinary Hospital. So Luke called and made an appointment.

What Luke didn't know was that Palmer had injured his spleen. If left untreated, Palmer would have had only hours to live.

Dr. Adrianne Becker just happened to be a Weimaraner lover—she had one of her own. She quickly realized what was going on, and made arrangements for the dog to be treated immediately at the city's famous Dove Lewis Emergency Animal Hospital. "Her diagnosis saved Palmer's life," says Luke.

But something more was happening during that assessment and examination. "I literally had an experience that I didn't believe could happen," says Luke. "I didn't believe in fate. But from the first time I saw Adrianne, I knew this was someone I could fall in love with."

Adrianne was feeling it too. She waived her medical fee for that initial examination. When someone at the hospital asked about it, she just smiled and said, "I have a hunch he'll be back."

Palmer's surgery at Dove Lewis was successful. Once Luke knew his dog was going to be OK, he asked the question that would change his life: Did he do follow-up visits with Dr. Becker or with the Dove Lewis staff? They said to follow up with his regular vet.

"That gave me two more opportunities to see her," says Luke.

Scientists now believe, based on genetic analysis, that dogs have been by our side for more than 100,000 years. When we were primitive cave dwellers our dogs were there, probably helping us hunt wooly mammoths. When the victorious hunter came back to camp, he probably impressed some sultry Cro-Magnon babe with all the clever tricks his dog could do.

They chatted during those visits. They found they were both from Michigan, and had actually dated people who were brother and sister. They both had Weimaraners, and both had also had Rottweilers.

Who would have thought Palmer's health emergency would bring Luke and Adrianne together?

It was the end of the last follow-up visit. Luke knew it was time to make his move. "I said something like, I could introduce her to some friends I'd made in Portland," he says. He was worried it sounded lame. Adrianne didn't think it sounded lame at all, and accepted his invitation.

That was seven months ago, and Adrianne and Luke have been a couple ever since. Her Weimaraner, Baloo, and her Rottweiler, Lynrd, have made friends with Palmer, and life is very good.

Oh, and Luke also found a job that fateful day he brought Palmer in for a veterinary visit. While he was in the waiting room, he picked up a copy of Dog Nose News, a community newspaper devoted to dogs. The paper was looking for an account executive to build up their advertising. Personable, smart, dog-loving Luke ended up being the perfect guy for the job.

You just never know what's going to happen when you take your dog to the vet.

Our dogs still share that incredible, glorious, magical bond with us. And, if we give them the chance, they can help us make that same connection with members of our own species.

Chapter 3

What Happens if This Book Falls Into the *Wrong Hands?*

Before I help you find love, a word of caution.

A friend of mine was horrified when I told her I was writing this book.

"What if the book falls into the *Wrong Hands?*" she demanded.

"The wrong hands?" I asked.

She nodded seriously.

"Like an armed robber or other evil-doer?"

"No," she answered darkly. It was obvious that the person with the *Wrong Hands* was worse than a mere homicidal maniac. "What if someone reads your book and gets a dog just to attract dates?" she asked.

Crimey! Even homicidal maniacs have more sense than that!

Let's add up what it costs to own a dog—and compare that with other ways you could use that money to attract members of the opposite sex.

The Cost of Dog Ownership

Most studies say that a typical dog owner spends about $500 a year to care for his or her dog.

Ha! Ha! Ha! If you're a serious dog owner, you are laughing now. For most of us, $500 a year is a mere down payment.

There are the dental appointments (you don't want a dog with periodontal disease—and the bad breath that comes with it). And there are training classes: obedience, agility, maybe something exotic like flyball or dancing with dogs. And the groomer. And the super-premium all-natural food, made with human-grade ingredients that cost six times as much as what you paid for your own dinner last night.

The expenses that can really put you in the poorhouse are the medical bills. Does your dog have a spinal problem? Make an appointment with a veterinary neurologist and a surgeon—and maybe even an acupuncturist and a chiropractor. Don't forget weeks at a specially designed doggie spa for physical rehabilitation.

There are doggie ophthalmologists, allergists, orthopedic surgeons, oncologists, cardiologists, reproductive specialists, dentists (who actually do doggie orthodontia) and even veterinary behaviorists—the canine equivalent of a psychiatrist. And they are not being paid by an HMO.

You'll want your dog to have the best of everything, from custom doggie beds to special training treats to rhinestone collars to Halloween costumes.

Expect to spend about $1,500 a year if you're a really devoted dog owner.

Because your dog is getting top-notch care, he'll live longer than most pets; a healthy, robust dog is likely to live to be 14 or over. Fourteen years at $1,500 a year—that's $21,000 over the life of your dog.

For $21,000 you can:

- Rent a Jaguar for three years or buy a Chrysler PT Cruiser and pay for insurance for four years. These cars are babe magnets and stud finders.

- Go to Harvard for eight months. Mentioning you went to Harvard is a sure-fire way to impress a member of the opposite sex.

- Rent a yacht and have the party of a lifetime—inviting every potential date you know.

- Buy the woman of your dreams a pair of diamond earrings (total carat weight of 2.0) from the Victoria collection at Tiffany and Company, and still have money to take her to a Broadway play and dinner at Sardi's.

- Buy the man you've got a crush on a Rolex Oyster President gold watch, and still have money left over to take him to an NBA play-off game.

- Get 14 Armani suits (for men or women). The corporate executive look just might catch the eye of someone else who's spending a fortune on clothes to attract an executive-type mate.

- Make yourself over with cosmetic surgery. For $21,000, you can buy liposuction, a tummy tuck, a facelift *and* breast augmentation (for women) or pectoral implants (for men).

So, if you're a non-dog person just looking for love, you can improve your odds by spending your money at the car dealership, Tiffany's, or maybe even the plastic surgeon's office.

If you're someone who is devoted to your dog but also wants to share your life with a dog-loving mate, this book is for you.

Chapter 4

The Best—and the Worst—Date Bait Breeds

While working on this book, dozens and dozens of people told me that their dog was a "chick magnet" or a "stud finder."

Name any task and you will find that dogs are not all created equal. Border Collies herd sheep better than Pekingese; Mastiffs make better guard dogs than Maltese; and a Miniature Pinscher fits on your lap better than a Doberman Pinscher.

And not all dogs make equal date bait. It's not always fair, but people respond differently to some breeds than they do to others. So, a list of the all-time best date bait breeds was inevitable. And so was a list of the worst.

The criterion for the best breeds was simple: These are the breeds that attract people. It doesn't mean they're smarter, nicer, easier to live with—it just means that if you walk these dogs, people are most likely to stop and talk with you and your dog. Conversely, the worst breeds are the ones people will actually walk away to avoid—or will stare at and shake their heads. Or make a rude remark.

After a year of interviewing scores of people, from dog experts to regular folks on the street, here are the long-awaited lists: the best and worst date bait breeds.

THE 10 BEST DATE BAIT BREEDS

1. **Golden Retriever.** Friendly and non-threatening, a Golden is the ideal date bait dog. With their happy faces, glistening fur and wagging tails, these dogs make humans feel good—and brave enough to say hello to the person at the end of the leash.

2. **Scruffy Terrier Mix.** Small terrier mixes can be the cutest dogs in the world. Bright eyes, an adventurous soul and the waifish tousle of hair compel people to come over and coo. Bonus points if the dog came from a shelter with a sad story—and has a fabulously happy life with you.

Puppies, Puppies, Puppies

Puppies of any breed attract attention. Scottish Terrier, Cocker Spaniel, Great Dane, Siberian Husky, Shih Tzu—it doesn't matter. Men and women will come over and caress the pup. They'll coo and kiss.

Of course, puppies grow up. Really fast. By the time a dog is six months old, he's looking like an adult. So the pull of puppies, while powerful, is fleeting.

Remember, puppyhood morphs into adolescence, the time when dogs lose their puppy cuteness and bounce off walls, jump on people, chew things to shreds. Don't expect puppy charms to last very long into your relationship.

You can't go wrong with a Golden Retriever (left) or a scruffy terrier mix. Both seem to make everyone feel good.

3. **Collie.** One word: Lassie. Who doesn't have childhood memories of yearning for this dog? Especially if you're looking for a love over 40, this dog will bring people to your side.

4. **Afghan Hound.** Elegant, aloof and hairy, this exotic breed isn't the kind of dog people will hug. However, they will stop in their tracks and say, "Wow!"

5. **Labrador Retriever.** There's a reason Labs are the number one dog in America—we just can't help but love these mugs. Half of America has a story about a Labrador they once loved, and will share it as they pet your dog.

6. **Pug.** Very hip thanks to the *Men in Black* movies, Pugs are friendly, happy, comical dogs who invite a conversation. They're small enough to be portable, but big enough to be sturdy pals. Note: At Pug parties around the globe, lots of people seem to feel compelled to dress their Pugs in clothes — especially giving female Pugs highly feminine

outfits, reminiscent of Miss Piggy. Don't dress your Pug in clothes if you're hoping to meet a normal human.

7. **Saint Bernard.** Nothing has quite the "awwwww" factor of a big, sweet, lovable Saint Bernard. They've got the big eyes and round heads that we're genetically programmed to respond to the way we respond to babies. They have giant size without intimidation, and are a guaranteed conversation starter. (Get used to people asking, "How much does that dog eat?!")

8. **Tiny Dogs With Big-Dog Confidence.** A lot of people are turned off by Yorkies, Maltese, Toy Poodles and other pint-sized pooches. However, if one of these tiny toy dogs is a confident, friendly little guy who looks people in the eye and sort of shrugs as if to say, "What's your problem?" you and your dog will soon have a small army of admirers.

9. **Beagle.** There's no friendlier face than a Beagle. This breed seems simple and straightforward, kind of a Midwestern working-guy dog in a convenient package.

10. **Old English Sheepdog.** Fuzzy, furry and funny, Old English Sheepdogs invite a hug. And you'll spend hours answering the question, "How does that dog see anything through all that hair?"

The Five Worst Date Bait Breeds

1. **Pit Bull.** There are lots of sweet, gentle Pit Bulls in the world, and most Pit Bulls love people and are great with kids. No matter how nice your Pit Bull may be, understand that, with the breed's fierce reputation, lots of people won't come near these dogs. Some communities have banned Pit Bulls and related breeds. Expect people to cross the street to avoid you if you have a Pit Bull, even if your dog is a wonderful, friendly, sweet soul.

2. **Rottweiler.** Like Pit Bulls, too often Rottweilers are given a bad rap, unfairly. These loyal, intelligent, trainable dogs can be fabulous pets for singles and families alike. But here's a hint: Any breed that is the subject of a cult classic movie named *Rottweiler: Dogs of Hell* may lose you more friends than it wins you.

3. **Yapping Little Dogs.** Some people don't like little dogs, period. *No one* likes yapping little dogs. These dogs can even irritate their owners.

4. **Dogs With Elaborate Hairdos.** People who show their Poodles learn to love all the fluff and pompons. Not the rest of the world. If your Poodle or other breed is trimmed like topiary, expect derisive laughter, not love.

5. **Chinese Crested.** These dogs are usually born naked, except for tufts of hair on their heads, feet and tails. No matter how smart, funny and just plain lovable these little guys are, even many of their owners admit they look a little bit like space aliens. It doesn't help that Chinese Crested are the perennial winner of the World's Ugliest Dog Contest, held annually in Petaluma, California. In fact, a Crested named Chi Chi is in the *Guinness Book of World Records* for winning this dubious title the most times—seven in all.

For Men (or Women) Only

While the appeal of some breeds, such as Golden Retrievers and Collies, is generally universal, other breeds have almost exclusive appeal to one gender, and usually not to the other:

Guy Breeds

Bulldog. Men relate to their big jowls and swagger. Women notice their gas.

Airedale. Called the "king of terriers," this big, brash dog is definitely a guy breed.

Boxer. Guy dog—and half of them are named after famous human boxers, like Tyson. Or underwear (as in Joe Boxer).

Chick Puppies

Shih Tzu. Women adore grooming them, just like they played with their baby dolls when they were kids. (And some empty nesters do seem to substitute a Shih Tzu for their grown-up children, and prefer them to their boisterous grandchildren.) Marissa agrees. "My daughter got her Shih Tzu when her youngest child started talking and playing outside. She had baby-itis and decided a Shih Tzu would need as much TLC as a baby and fix the 'itch.' She was right! Annie is a little doll baby . . . and takes plenty of mothering."

Toy Poodle. Tiny, delicate, sensitive and requires grooming: This dog is for women only. And it shouldn't surprise you that these dogs often have names like Prada and Chanel.

Shetland Sheepdog: A Sheltie looks a lot like a Collie in miniature, but Collies are equally a woman's and a man's dog. Shelties are solely a chick breed.

Sometimes Size Does Matter

When it comes to doggie dating, size usually matters. Men generally prefer big, athletic, brawny dogs. Women more often want dogs that fit on their lap—and sometimes in their purse. So if you're a man who wants to attract a woman, you'll want a small, sweet, sensitive dog. And a woman just might want to be walking a studly-looking big dog.

What's So Attractive About Little Dogs and Men?

If you're a strong-looking man, it melts a woman's heart to see you acting gentle enough to care for a little, sweet, sensitive dog. A few years ago, there were news reports from Japan that one entrepreneur was renting out small dogs to men, to help them attract women.

What effect does a man with a small, sweet dog have on a woman? Just ask Patrice. "My dream man would have a Sheltie," she says with a far-away look in her eye. "It takes a gentle, sensitive person to bond with a Sheltie."

More often than not, however, men aren't attracted to a woman with a small dog. "Men think that women with lap dogs want a baby," says Nikki.

Attracting Bad Boys

If you're a woman walking a macho breed, you'll meet a lot of men. "The problem is that a lot of these guys are scary," says one woman who has Doberman Pinschers. "Guys who like them tend to be criminals." A woman with a Pit Bull agrees. "Sometimes they start talking about their guns," she says. At least you *will* meet men.

If you're a macho-looking man walking a macho-looking dog, don't be stunned when you don't attract a lot of women. Just like—for reasons you may not understand—you're not attracting them with your pick-up with the gun rack on the back.

Looking for Special Someone

Today, everything is about niche markets. Television has learned that lesson: We have a hundred cable channels and each aims for different demographics—everything from the Food Channel to MTV to the History Channel to Animal Planet has its own audience.

We usually admire in a dog those things that we admire—or strive for—in ourselves. So, if you're running 20 miles a week, you'll probably admire a dog who's equally athletic and fit. If you're looking for a special kind of person, you might be best served by a special kind of dog.

For example:

> **The Liberal Left-of-Center Urban Hipster.** Forget all the purebreds on the 10 Best List. You need a dog from a shelter. How important is this? When John F. Kennedy, Jr. bought a purebred Canaan Dog, he told people it was a shelter mix. The dog's true identity didn't come out until Kennedy's death, when dog lovers worried about what became of the pooch, and the breeder had to step forward and say that the supposed shelter dog was alive and well with her. (Another lesson here: Don't fib!)
>
> **Outdoorsy Love Interest.** If you're looking for a hunting, fishing, outdoorsy man or woman, you're not likely to meet this person while you're walking your Pekingese. (Especially since most Pekingese can only walk a block or so.) An athletic German Shorthaired Pointer would be a better choice.
>
> **Non-conformist.** You'll want a dog that goes beyond mixed—think of a lovable mutt who looks like he was designed by a committee. Maybe stubby legs (like a Corgi) and the slender face of a Greyhound—and patches of hair of different lengths and textures. This dog isn't going to conform to anybody's breed standard.
>
> **Mental Health Professional.** One Basenji breeder claims that a disproportionate number of psychiatrists own this fastidiously clean, barkless breed.

What to Do if the Dog You Love Isn't on the List

Yikes! There's a good chance your dog didn't make the 10 Best List. Or, worse yet, made the Five Worst List. Not to worry! With a little help from you, your dog can be a canine ambassador—and attract new friends to you and to his breed.

*Winston is an American Staffordshire Terrier, a tough-looking dog.
But how can you be afraid of a really buff guy wearing formal
attire and bringing you flowers?*

If Your Dog Looks Scary

If you've got a big, brawny, scary-looking dog, soften his looks. The easiest, most effective way: a cool bandana around his neck. If he's kind of a lovable goofball, maybe he wouldn't even mind wearing a sun visor and sunglasses in summer. These tiny cosmetic changes have an enormous impact on how people view your dog.

If Your Dog Is Very Little or Looks Weird

Train your dog. People admire a dog who is very well trained—one who sits when you stop, does tricks, works on hand signals (see the Appendix for more information on training).

Much of the resistance to very little dogs, very big dogs and odd-looking dogs is old-fashioned prejudice. These people decide they don't like your dog without ever meeting him, and for no reason. What you'll learn when you help people overcome this prejudice by showing off your well-trained dog is that the dog's biggest detractors will turn into his biggest fans. They won't just think he's smart, they'll think he's the *smartest dog in the world.* And he's not just friendly, he's the *most lovable dog in history.* That's the positive side of overcoming prejudice—it turns into adoration.

Carrying a Toy

Lots of dogs like to carry toys with them on walks. If you have a dog who looks scary or a little dog, you'd be amazed how people respond to the dog showing his teddy bear to everyone. (Of course, this only works if the dog likes to share his teddy bear. If he growls and stares balefully at the person admiring the toy, this isn't good. Not good at all.)

Dogs Who Play Golf and Soccer

Here are some true stories about how people's views about a dog change just by what he does. My dog Radar is a seven-pound Papillon—a little black and white dog with huge ears that look like butterfly wings. Although Radar has several obedience titles to his credit, men were mostly unimpressed by this butterfly dog. Until he played golf.

A local television station decided to develop a fake commercial, in which viewers could supposedly buy "pup putts"—golfing gadgets that would improve your score. I trained Radar to grab a golf ball and drop it into the hole when I said, "Make par!"

During training (which I did on a putting practice area at a local golf course) and during filming, Radar's golf game turned quite a few heads. This demographically desirable group of men—who would normally have been nonplussed by a dog who has been described as "a cat in drag"—were fascinated by the way he played their game. After one practice session, a man came up, looked at Radar in admiration, and said, "That is a great dog."

I knew a Pit Bull who always carried a soccer ball when he went for walks. When kids (or attractive women) came up, the man who owned the dog would ask them to throw the dog's ball. The dog would kick the ball back, and the dog and the woman would play soccer. Suddenly, instead of being a big, scary Pit Bull, this great dog was a fun soccer buddy.

Sports companies have said for years that the truly hip play sports. Apparently, if your dog plays sports, he's viewed as more cool—and probably more human—than other dogs.

Your dog doesn't have to be the canine equivalent of Michael Jordan. Bring along a Frisbee or a tennis ball for him to chase and people will volunteer to throw it. When they experience the joy of playing fetch with a great dog, they forget to hate the dog.

If You Have a Poodle

Poodles of all three sizes (toy, miniature and standard) are handsome, athletic, intelligent dogs—and some of the most highly trainable animals in dogdom. What everyone makes fun of is the hairdo. There's nothing in this world that says you have to decorate your Poodle with pompons. One of the most handsome dogs I've ever seen was a Standard Poodle whose coat was cut evenly all over, about half an inch long. This included the tail: no fancy pompon. The dog's owner spent huge amounts of time convincing people this was really a Poodle. Groomed without frills, the dog looked more like the sporting dog this breed used to be.

The other alternative is to embrace the frills. There used to be a woman who jogged through my neighborhood with her black Standard Poodle. The dog was in full show coat: huge billows of hair on his head and chest, and shaved naked on his butt and legs (except for those decorative pompons). The woman who jogged with him always wore a black, fluffy, faux fur jacket that just came to her waist, and skin-tight black leggings. Yes, the dog and owner looked like they were wearing matching outfits. But they were both beautiful and athletic. People couldn't help but stand still and watch them jog by with their elegant strides. In that instance, it worked to embrace the weirdness.

The Real Top of the List

It's fun to think about which dogs attract the most attention, and it's not a bad idea to think of ways to make your dog seem less threatening or less weird to people you meet.

But the dog who's at the real top of the date bait list is the dog you love. The dog you trust with your soul, and who trusts you right back with all his heart.

That relationship shows. When someone sees how kind you are with your dog, and sees how much your dog adores you—that's when the magic between you can spread to another human. You can't buy that by getting a certain breed of dog. You can't fake it with a dog who isn't your soulmate.

Nothing attracts love like love.

Chapter 5

So Your Dog Isn't a Party Animal

Some of us are extroverts. We love to meet new people, try out the latest hot spots and go with the flow. But some of us are introverts. We feel uncomfortable in unfamiliar surroundings and we feel shy around new people.

Some of us have dogs who love us, but may react fearfully or aggressively toward other people or other dogs.

There are some things you can do to help your dog. And who knows, you just might find a human soulmate along the way.

Shy Dogs

About 15 percent of people and dogs are shy (defined as uncomfortable with unfamiliar places or people). Sometimes the people who have shy dogs—often rescuing them from sad situations—are shy themselves. These kind souls take these dogs because of the special empathy they feel.

So . . . you've got a shy owner and a shy dog. I bet you're thinking this doesn't sound like a recipe for success in meeting the perfect mate. You're wrong.

People who own shy dogs soon learn that the most important antidote to shyness is gentle, loving, non-threatening exposure to safe new people and safe new situations. While a happy-go-lucky dog might do fine just playing with neighborhood kids in your backyard, over time a shy dog needs to be taken into the real world or she will just get worse. Over the years, you'll probably end up going more places and meeting more people with your shy dog than anyone you know who has a "normal" dog.

Here are a few rules to help your shy dog adjust to new social situations (and a few hints for the shy owner, as well).

Don't overwhelm your shy dog. It's important to expose your dog to new places and new things, but it's equally important not to flood her with stimulation. Take her to small neighborhood parks, not a crowded shopping center. Walk with her quietly; don't let her get mugged by the dogs at the dog park.

Carry food. Most people will reach out to pet your shy dog. An outstretched hand coming over a dog's head is the scariest gesture a human can make, and it will terrify most shy dogs. Instead, carry yummy, gooey, smelly, delicious (to a dog) treats with you. When someone wants to pet your dog, explain that your dog is shy, but it would be great if the person would give your pooch one of these special treats. A true dog lover will be thrilled to take the gooey, slimy, smelly treat and give it to your shy dog.

Develop your own patter. Dog talent agent Paula Ratoza has a shy Doberman Pinscher who was abused before she adopted him. She says people would often make nasty comments to her, assuming his "hang dog" look was her fault. She learned to explain her dog's history and asked people to give him a treat. When they gave him a treat, Paula would tell Higgins "head up" and he'd hold his head up tall and proud as he took the treat. Now he knows the commands "head up" and also "head down"—recreating his old, sad look. This comes in handy when this now happy dog has a role in a television commercial.

Love your shy dog, take her places, build her confidence, and watch her blossom into a happier, more relaxed pet. Just think: The next person who helps you by giving your dog a slimy dog treat might be the kind, sweet soul who will be your perfect match. Don't be surprised if this new dream date is just a little bit shy. After all, a shy person has the empathy and heart to understand what your dog is going through.

(For more about shy dogs, read *Help for Your Shy Dog: Turning Your Terrified Dog Into a Terrific Pet,* by Deborah Wood—who else?)

Aggressive Dogs

Aggression is the most troubling problem that comes between people and their pets. If you have a dog who isn't safe with other people or dogs, or may have attacked you, this dog is not date bait. In fact, you need to address your dog's aggression before you focus on your own love life. If you don't address this right away, it will only get worse.

Here are a few ideas that might help:

Find a trainer or behaviorist who uses gentle methods. Far more often than not, if you treat aggression with force, the problem will escalate. This trainer will probably have you follow a plan in which your dog has to work for a living: Every time you give him food, or even a gentle pat, he needs to sit, lie down, or do something else to show that he's earning his keep. (The thinking goes that in the wild, the top dog in the

When Pepper Found the Right Party

Sometimes the trick is finding the place where your grouchy dog is happy. Writer Nikki Moustaki has a rescued Miniature Schnauzer that even she admits can be a little on the cranky side. "The most common thing people said was, 'Get him away from me!'" admits Nikki. "Pepper repelled people. We were outcasts." The problem: Pepper is reactive to movement. When he sees a skateboard or kids running or other sudden movement, he reacts to the excitement by barking and lunging.

But when Nikki took Pepper to a formal dinner put on by a dog food company, the dog was a star. "I was dressed in an evening gown, and was carrying Pepper. He loved it! He was so good. Some guy said, 'There's a cute dog and a cute girl,'" says Nikki, with a laugh.

The difference: This elegant dinner didn't include any of Pepper's triggers. There weren't loud kids in the room, and no skateboards whizzing past. Pepper had a chance to show the side of him that Nikki loves.

Sometimes it's a matter of knowing your dog and finding his place to shine.

pack controls who gets food and attention. When the dog has to work for you to get food and attention, he views you as the big dog in charge, and treats you with more respect.)

 Teach your dog "watch me." Your dog can't get into fights or attack people if he's looking at you. Dogs' bodies follow their eyes. Teach your dog "watch me" by holding a treat in front of your eyes. When he stares longingly at your face, say "Good watch me!" and give him the treat. Over time, hold the treat in your hand but only reward the dog when he looks in your eyes. Build up the length of time of the eye contact, so you can ask your dog to "watch me" when trouble comes near, and he will focus on you until the temptation has passed.

Use a head collar. Head collars (brands such as Halti Collar and Gentle Leader) fit over your dog's head, just like a halter fits on a horse. Just as you can lead a horse wherever you want to go with a halter, so you can lead even a big dog with a head collar. In addition, the feeling of the strap over the dog's nose is something like the way a top dog gently nuzzles the muzzle of a lower-ranking dog, so over and over the head collar is telling your dog that you're the boss—and he isn't. Sometimes that gentle reminder will make an almost magical difference in a dog.

Know your dog. Know what triggers your dog, and avoid those situations. So if he's dog-aggressive, don't take him to the dog park: That's just asking for an awful incident. If he growls when people come within four feet—stay five feet away.

With expert help and a lot of patience, your aggressive dog might turn the corner and become a safe, reliable citizen. And with all the dog trainers you'll be meeting, you never know where you'll find love.

Chapter 6

Using the Techniques of Dog Experts and the Secrets of the AKC to Find the Perfect Human Mate

Most dog lovers find the perfect match—at least of the four-legged kind. I don't know anyone who regrets which dog they slept with last night. The same can't always be said of the human in the bed. Let's face it: Most of us are far better at picking the perfect pooch than at finding the ideal mate.

Take Barbara, for example. And take her ex-husband—*please*. Barbara knew exactly what she wanted in a dog. She picked active, intense Indy, an Australian Shepherd puppy, and never regretted it.

Indy is a whiz at obedience training—earning a Utility Degree, sort of the doggie equivalent of a Ph.D. He's also an ace at tracking, earning an American Kennel Club title in which he had to follow the trail of a stranger through thick brush and over a stream. Indy is now 13 years old, and he and Barbara couldn't be more closely bonded.

Ah, if things had only gone so well with Barbara's marriage. Ted was a handsome, slow-moving, unmotivated, gentle, blue-collar guy. Kind of the human equivalent of a Basset Hound. Within months of the marriage, high-powered Barbara found herself constantly picking at poor Ted. She wanted him to have more ambition, more energy. In less than two years, the couple wisely decided to go their separate ways.

If only Barbara had used the same thought process in picking Ted as she did with Indy. I mean *exactly* the same thought process.

The experts will tell you that there isn't a right breed of dog or a wrong breed of dog—there's just the right and wrong breed for *you*.

It's the same with picking a mate. There's nothing wrong with falling in love with a high-powered executive—unless you want a mate who will spend time with you on weekends. And there's nothing wrong with a school teacher—unless you want to own a yacht. You just need to find the right long-term love for your lifestyle.

Use the same criteria to pick a mate as you use to pick a dog—and you'll find surprising success!

The Basic Categories

Check out any book on picking the right breed of dog and it will give you consistent categories to consider. Apply them to humans and you won't make so many mistakes.

City/Suburban/Country

Some dogs and people are meant to enjoy the crowds of city living, others need the wide-open spaces of the country.

The Dog Version: Pekingese make great city dogs; they think a walk across the living room floor is aerobic exercise. Border Collies aren't happy without a flock of sheep.

The Human Version: Ask a forest ranger to sit still through an opera and he's likely to end up just as wacko as a Border Collie cooped up in a condo. Give an urban professional a weekend without a cell phone and she'll need extra daily therapy sessions for a year.

High Drive vs. Couch Potato

We acknowledge that some breeds are hard-wired to work and some are just built for snuggling. We accept this better in dogs than we do in humans.

The Dog Version: A Jack Russell Terrier wants to dig and chase; this dog never rests. A Coonhound sleeps until a raccoon wakes him up. These two dogs may both hunt vermin, but they're hardly the same species.

The Human Version: The human version of the Jack Russell might be the advertising executive works 80 hours a week and vacations with a laptop, fax machine and Palm Pilot at hand. The human Coonhound is the free spirit who lives in a mobile home, has a part-time job as a night watchman and dreams of the murder mystery he's going to write someday. Just not today.

Independence vs. Dependence

Some of us want a constant companion. Others need space to breathe.

The Dog Version: Papillons are so devoted to their owners, they'll sit and watch them in the toilet. Basenjis are cat-like in their independence.

The Human Version: Some people call up their lovers on the phone five times a day. Others happily take separate vacations.

Good With Kids?

Every book on selecting the right dog rates the breeds on how well they play with children. Have you ever applied the same question to a potential spouse?

> **The Dog Version:** A typical Golden Retriever will play fetch with his favorite five-year-old for hours, his soft, sweet eyes shining with joy. A small, spindly Italian Greyhound looks at a child with revulsion—she practically shudders at the sight of anyone who isn't old enough to order an extra-dry martini.
>
> **The Human Version:** The tall, spindly woman who practically shudders at the sight of anyone who isn't old enough to order an extra-dry martini—and the guy who volunteers his time as a coach to city teams, even though he doesn't have children.

Maintenance

Admit it: Some of us require an entourage, others are good to go in five minutes.

> **The Dog Version:** Poodles and Bichons Frises require regular, pricey visits to the groomer. And then there are Komondors and Pulis—dogs who have hair that is painstakingly twisted into long dreadlocks.
>
> **The Human Version:** Not only do some humans require pricey treatments at hair stylists, massage therapists and pedicurists—many need constant hours of ego stroking. We've all known high-maintenance people, and they all require more work than any dog.

The Practical Application

Use the same intelligence picking out a mate that you used selecting your practically perfect dog. Think about what you admire most in your favorite breeds and apply those traits to the human you want to meet.

Here's a chart to get you started:

Dog Breed	Characteristics	Human Counterpart
Jack Russell Terrier	Independent, industrious, can't be forced to do anything want she doesn't to do	Small business owner, maybe a home builder
Newfoundland	Gentle, hard-working, giants, Newfoundlands are workaholics; they love to pull kids on carts, perform water rescue (owners have to pretend to drown), and visit sick kids	Pediatrician
Border Collie	Always busy, always thinking, these dogs have trouble coping if they don't have a job to do	This is the kid who was labeled as Attention Deficit Disorder in school and grows up to have four or five simultaneous successful jobs; this person never sleeps
Rottweiler	Loyal guardian, always vigilant, blue collar dog.	Police officer
Golden Retriever	Great with kids, mellow but smart, always has a smile on his face	Grade school teacher
Borzoi	Leggy and lean, exotic in her beauty, a Borzoi has an aesthetic of her own	Artist, actor
Shetland Sheepdog	Gentle and soft, very in tune with people	Counselor, psychologist
Miniature Pinscher	Small and sharp, this tiny breed is sure that he is much tougher than his small size indicates	Executive secretary to the head of a large corporation
Labrador Retriever	Easygoing and gentle, most Labradors get along well with humans and other dogs	Veterinarian
Basset Hound	Long and laid-back, most Bassets go at their own pace—slow	Plumber, being paid by the hour
Doberman Pinscher	Clever, driven, protective	District attorney
Standard Poodle	Smart, empathetic, glamorous, high maintenance	Advertising executive

Just the Right Words

Describe the dog of your dreams. Does this description apply to people you've been dating lately? If not, maybe you're barking up the wrong tree when it comes to love.

At a loss for words in describing your perfect mate? The American Kennel Club has some adjectives that might come in handy. Every purebred dog has an AKC breed standard that describes the looks and temperament of that breed. If you're at a loss for words in describing the human of your dreams, check out these descriptions!

> **German Shepherd Dog:** ". . . giving the impression, both at rest and in motion, of muscular fitness and nimbleness without any look of clumsiness or soft living . . . stamped with a look of quality and nobility—difficult to define, but unmistakable when present."
>
> **Pembroke Welsh Corgi:** "Outlook bold, but kindly. Expression intelligent and interested. Never shy nor vicious."
>
> **Scottish Terrier:** ". . . very special keen, piercing, 'varminty' expression. . . ."
>
> **Bulldog:** "The disposition should be equable and kind, resolute and courageous. . . ."
>
> **Affenpinscher:** ". . . described as the *diablotin moustachu* or the mustached little devil."
>
> **Mastiff:** "The impression is one of grandeur and dignity."
>
> **Pomeranian:** "He is alert in character, exhibits intelligence in expression, is buoyant in deportment, and inquisitive by nature . . . cocky, commanding and animated. . . .
>
> **Siberian Husky:** "The males . . . are masculine but never coarse, the bitches are feminine without weakness. . . ."
>
> **Basset Hound:** ". . . extreme in its devotion."
>
> **Cocker Spaniel:** "Above all, he must be free and merry. . . ."

Irish Terrier: "There is a heedless, reckless pluck . . . which is characteristic, and which, coupled with the headlong dash, blind to all consequences, with which he rushes at his adversary, has earned . . . the proud epithet of 'Daredevil.'"

Golden Retriever: ". . . displaying a kindly expression and possessing a personality that is eager, alert and self-confident."

Go fetch! Put as much thought into finding a mate as you do into finding a dog, and you might find a human in your bed who's a perfect match.

Chapter 7

A Healthy Balance

Life is best when we're in balance. We respect our dogs and we respect ourselves. We have room in our life for other people, but still take time for our own needs. People who are in balance attract more relationships—and the relationships they attract are healthier.

Here's your chance to take a quiz! Heck, if *Cosmopolitan* magazine can give monthly quizzes (and they don't know a thing about dogs), a dog trainer can certainly design a dating quiz. This one tests how well balanced your relationship is with your dog—and the implications of adding a human to your household.

Quiz

Is Your Relationship With Your Dog Out of Balance?

1. You and your pooch are out for a walk. You:

   a. Look fabulous, but can't remember the last time the dog had a bath.

    b. Didn't quite get around to brushing your hair this morning, but your dog has already had his whiskers trimmed, his pedicure and his teeth brushed. (Oops! Did you remember to brush *your* teeth?)

    c. Both look pretty darn good, considering your ages.

2. Your dog:

    a. Has the longest pedigree money can buy—you always buy the best of everything.

    b. Is a dog—who can remember what breed(s)? After all, they're all the same under the fur.

    c. Is the perfect size and energy level for your lifestyle.

3. When it comes to buying dog food:

    a. You buy whatever is on sale. After all, this isn't rocket science—it's *dog food.*

    b. You read the label, and both you and your dog eat healthy, well-balanced food. OK—maybe an occasional snack.

    c. You go to the pricey organic grocery for the dog's food, and then go to the mega-grocery and get junk food and comfort food for yourself. Well, at least the dog eats right!

4. When it comes to health care:

    a. Your dog has veterinary health insurance, but you can't afford the premiums for human health coverage. You're hoping all those dog walks keep you healthy!

    b. You love your dog, but you just can't see going in debt for a dog. After all, it's not like he's going to live forever.

    c. You both get plenty of exercise and eat well, and get your regularly scheduled physicals. If your dog really needed an expensive procedure, you'd figure out a way to pay for it—even if it meant getting a paper route.

5. When it comes to time together:

   a. You must admit you feel pretty guilty. You know you should be home more for your dog. He really needs more exercise. Maybe next month, after the big project is over.

   b. You go to obedience class and to the dog park, where you both have lots of buddies. Other times, he sits on your lap while you read a novel. You don't feel guilty when you go see a movie with some two-legged friends.

   c. The dog sets the schedule. You just follow it.

6. At night . . .

   a. He sleeps in the middle of the bed, and you hang precariously to the corner of the bed. And he gets all the covers, too. If you move, he growls and means it.

   b. Of course he sleeps in the bed. You're both happier that way.

   c. He's a pain in the butt, what with all the whining and the moving around. He sleeps in the basement, and you stretch out on the king-size bed and get a real night's sleep.

7. If you got an out-of-town job offer:

   a. You'd take it in a second if it's right for your career. If your dog has to live with your mom for a year or two, he'll be fine.

   b. You would never move under any conditions—you can't imagine another situation that would work as well for your dog as the one you have now.

   c. You and your dog would have to adjust to the new city, but you'd have fun exploring it together. He'd have a bunch of new fire hydrants to mark, and you'd have a whole new set of stores to browse.

8. You consider your dog:

   a. Your pet.

   b. An important, beloved family member.

   c. A major deity.

Scoring

1.	a. 3	b. 1	c. 2
2.	a. 3	b. 1	c. 2
3.	a. 1	b. 2	c. 3
4.	a. 1	b. 3	c. 2
5.	a. 3	b. 2	c.1
6.	a. 1	b. 2	c. 3
7.	a. 3	b. 1	c. 2
8.	a. 3	b. 2	c. 1

Your Score

18-24: It's all about you—and not enough about your dog. Your dog needs time, attention and love, and he's not getting enough of it. Dogs aren't mere possessions; they're living, breathing, loving creatures who need to have that love and adoration returned. Adding a human love interest to your life right now will only take time away from your dog, and that's not what he needs. Give your dog more of a priority in your life and you'll both be a lot happier.

12-17: You and your dog are an awesome team. You're in a healthy place, both mentally and physically. Your love for each other shines though, and you're attractive to other dog lovers. Let the good times roll (over)!

0-11: Right now you aren't treating yourself with as much dignity and respect as you treat your dog. With all the time you're spending on your dog, there isn't any room for you—much less a love interest. Life is healthiest when there's a balance, and you need to find it. Your dog will be a happier dog when he's part of a pack, and not the king of the house. You'll also be more appealing to other humans when you have the self-esteem to take care of yourself. So make a resolution: Whatever you do for your dog, do for yourself, as well. Your dog will still be happy, and you'll feel better and gain confidence.

When a Good Idea Goes Over the Top

A friend of mine has a motto: Anything worth doing is worth doing to excess. Of course, that philosophy landed my friend in a lot of trouble (until he got clean and sober). In real life, extremes are hardly ever a good idea.

Sometimes you have a perfectly good idea, but you take it just a little too far. Because we're so head-over-heels in love with our dogs, sometimes we don't know where to draw the line. We need a little help.

Here's a chart that shows what's hot—and what's over the top.

What's Hot	What's Over the Top
A bandana around your dog's neck	A faux fur coat and a matching pillbox hat
Adopting a dog from the shelter	Calling her your adopted daughter (worse yet is asking people not to tell the dog that she's adopted)
Talking with your dog	Talking with your dog in baby talk ("My itty bitty Boobsie wuvs her dada!")
Keeping your dog sparkling clean	Putting perfume on your dog—even perfume made for dogs. Especially perfume made for dogs.
Naming your dog a people name (Sophie and Max far outnumber Princess and Spot in the doggie set)	Naming your dog after your mother
A T-shirt with a picture of your dog's breed on it	Matching outfits for you and your dog (mother-daughter clothing isn't even attractive on people)
Looking like your dog	Dying your hair to look more like your dog

However, mother-daughter outfits never looked good on anyone.

A cool bandana around your dog's neck is always in style.

Why Balance Matters

You don't think balance matters? Here's a true story:

Courtney was attracted to Mike from the beginning. They were both animal lovers, and were volunteering at their local shelter. They were just out of college, and neither had a dog at the time.

But the dating didn't go well. "He wasn't very considerate, and we broke up after a time. I thought he was a jerk," admits Courtney.

A couple of weeks later, Mike called and made an admission: Courtney's instincts were right. He had been a jerk. The whole time they'd been dating, he had been seeing another woman. "He called to say he'd ended the other relationship and wanted just to date me," says Courtney. "I hesitated, but he was being open and honest."

Then Mike said something that appealed to Courtney. "He told me he had a new Sheltie." That sealed the deal; a guy with a Sheltie couldn't be all bad. Courtney agreed to see Mike again.

"At the end of the date, Mike was going to drive me home, about 25 miles. He asked if I'd mind having the dog come along. Since the only reason I agreed to date him again was because he had a dog, I said it would be great to have the dog come along."

Then the other shoe dropped. "Mike brought the dog to the car, and explained that the dog likes to ride in the front seat. I needed to sit in the back. So, for the whole ride home, there I am in the back seat and the dog is riding in the front, enjoying the view. I couldn't believe this was the make-up date."

That was also the last date. The moral of the story: balance, balance, balance. Courtney just wanted to be treated as well as Mike treated his dog. That isn't too much to ask.

By the way, Courtney later married an architect. One year his anniversary gift to her was a giant playhouse for her cats, which she thought was the most romantic gift she had ever received.

Chapter 8

Dogs as Date Bait in Film and Fiction

Sometimes you just don't feel like going out. You want to sit at home, share the couch with your dog and watch a good video or read an entertaining book.

Not to worry! There are several with doggie date bait themes. Here's the good, the bad and the ugly.

Movies

🐾 🐾 🐾 🐾 *The Accidental Tourist.* Well, technically this isn't a film about using your dog as date bait, but it's way better than any of the films on the subject. Macon Leary (played by William Hurt) writes travel books for people who want to avoid human contact. He falls in love with wacky dog trainer Muriel Pritchett (Geena Davis), and chooses her over his ex-wife, Sarah (Kathleen Turner). (Any movie where the wacky dog trainer is the main love interest is worthwhile cinema!)

This movie contains one of the great cinematic dog moments of all time. Pritchett's odd little son is being teased by other children. He walks away, in obvious pain—and Leary unleashes his Cardigan Welsh Corgi to run to the boy's side. It's a moment of gentleness, healing and power.

Paws way, way up for this thinking person's classic. (Warner Brothers, 1989, Rated PG)

🐾 🐾 🐾 *The Truth About Cats and Dogs.* Abby Barnes (Janeane Garofalo) is a veterinarian who has a pet advice radio show. After she takes a call to help out photographer Brian (Ben Chaplin), who is having trouble with a roller-skating dog, the handsome guy asks her out. The problem: She tells him she's a tall, beautiful blonde. Soon she recruits neighbor Noelle Slusarsky (Uma Thurman) to date the guy— and then both women decide they want him.

It's a goofy premise. You'd think the guy would notice that Garofalo sounds totally different in real life than she does on the radio or phone, and that the blonde substitute has only half the I.Q. Still, it's an engaging, sweet film if you suspend your disbelief just a little.

This movie shows a genuine fondness for animals. And the advice Abby gives on air: it's right on the money!

Paws up! (20th Century Fox, 1996, rated PG)

🐾 🐾 🐾 *Turner and Hooch.* OK, this movie is really more of a cop buddy movie, with Tom Hanks playing Scott Turner, the neurotic, brainy, ambitious cop, and drooling, gaseous Hooch (a Dogue de Bordeaux) as the street-smart cop, Hooch. But Hanks does fall in love with a veterinarian, and Hooch does fall in love with her Collie.

This movie is an endearing classic that we'll still be watching 50 years from now. Big, drooly Dogue de Bordeaux paws up for this one! (Touchstone, 1989, rated PG)

🐾 🐾 *Just a Walk in the Park.* In this made-for-TV movie, Manhattan dog walker Adam (George Eads) falls in love with Rachel (Jane Krakowski) while he's dog-sitting for a millionaire. Of course, she thinks he's actually the wealthy guy he is dog-sitting for.

While there's not a single surprise in this romantic comedy, it still has its charms—including the fact that the dog walker gets the gorgeous woman. The actors have a lot of appeal, which makes this silly movie a guilty delight.

Paws up—as long as you're not in the mood for Shakespeare. (ABC Family Channel, 2002, not rated)

🐾 *Dog Park.* This isn't only one of the worst dog-related movies ever made, it's on the short list of least interesting movies *ever*. The movie tracks seven singles looking for love at the dog park. I couldn't even keep the dogs straight, much less their insipid, vain and selfish owners. Even the racy scenes weren't any fun, because I really didn't want to know any of these people.

Paws way, way down—use the pooper scooper on this one. (New Line Cinema, 1999, rated R)

Books

The Wicked Flea by Susan Conant. (Berkley, $22.95, 289 pages) is the 14th book in this popular dog lover's mystery series.. In this one, Holly Winter's veterinarian boyfriend has married someone else—so Holly is looking for love (not to mention a new vet). A friend tells her to check out the local dog park to meet single dog lovers, but of course, soon one of the dog walkers ends up dead.

In the funniest parts of this entertaining book, you'll read the notes of the psychiatrist who is helping Holly through her break-up with her boyfriend. When the psychiatrist finds that Holly goes dancing with her dog (not to mention that she insists that dogs are people) the therapist concludes that Holly has some serious problems.

If you're looking for a tightly plotted mystery, don't turn to Conant's books. On the other hand, if you want a fun read that captures the soul of a dog lover, this 2002 installment in the Holly Winter series is for you.

Finding Mr. Right by Emily Carmichael (Bantam Books, $5.50, 368 pages) is hilarious. It's the story of a woman who was having an affair with her best friend's husband, but was shot by a robber when she and her boyfriend were out on a date. She comes back to earth as an overweight rescue Corgi whose job it is to find a new husband for her best friend. This book is clever, funny and sharp-edged—not what you'd expect in a romance novel. Even hard-core mystery readers will enjoy this one.

Diamond in the Ruff, also by Emily Carmichael (Bantam, $5.50, 416 pages), is the sequel to *Finding Mr. Right.* Although it's an entertaining read, it isn't as edgy as its predecessor—more of a romance and less of a mystery.

Chapter 9

Train Your Dog to Fetch a Date

They say that dogs never lie about love. Maybe that's true, but they can help you fib a little. Teach your dog some tricks and you'll have some fun with him, and just might impress a few people. (There is an Appendix at the end of this book with some hints for successful training. It will help you teach your dogs these tricks, and lots of others. That section also includes some recommended reading for trick training.)

Sneaky Tricks for Devious People

Since you're still reading this section, now we know something about you! Here are some practical—OK, and some not so practical—ways to enlist your dog to help you find Mr. or Ms. Right.

Limp

This one works on people in helping professions, such as doctors and nurses. It's a perfect trick to practice when you're taking your dog for a stroll in front of a hospital.

> **The Skill:** The dog holds one of his front paws in the air, hobbling on three feet. You exclaim, "Oh my poor dog seems to be limping!" (Of course, when the kindly doctor comes over to help, grab the dog's paw and pretend to pull a little pebble from his pad—so he's cured, and you've got an attractive doctor to visit with.)
>
> **How to Teach It:** Put the dog's leash under one of his front legs, holding the leg gently off the ground. Ask him to step toward you, saying, "Good limp!" and still holding his leg in place with his leash. Very quickly, your dog will learn to hold his foot above the leash and "limp" toward you. Over time, put the leash closer and closer to the ground, still asking the dog to limp—and eventually he'll do the trick when he doesn't have his leash on. (For a detailed description of the training techniques for this trick, see the Appendix.)

Fetching From the Herd

A herding dog can bring a farmer a single sheep from a huge herd. Your dog can bring you back one date from a gaggle of potential lovers. Who says dogs aren't man's (and woman's) best friends?

> **The Skill:** This trick has two parts: The dog goes to a person you point to, and then herds that person back to you. This trick capitalizes on the natural behavior of some dogs, especially the herding breeds. If you have a dog who naturally brings things to you, especially if he's a dog who can move your cat from room to room, you can work up to telling him to bring objects—and people—to you.

Lassie, fetch that guy!

How to Teach It: Part one is teaching your dog to go to someone you point to. The easiest way to teach this is in cooperation with a few friends. Have a friend hold a treat in her hand. Make sure the dog sees the treat. Then point to your friend as you release the dog and say a cue word, such as "gorgeous." Quickly, he'll run to your friend every time you say "gorgeous." Make sure your friend gives him the treat and lots of praise.

Once he runs to your friend on command, practice the command with other friends. This way, your dog will understand that he's supposed to run to get a treat from whomever you're pointing to—not just a specific person.

Part two relies on natural behavior. If you have a dog who likes to herd, you'll realize he's nudging all kinds of things your way: the cat, balls that are too big to pick up, even your kids. Encourage that behavior by saying, "Good bring back!" "Yes, good bring back!" Your herding dog will quickly engage in the game, and will start nudging even more stray things to you and will think it's fun.

Then, combine the commands. Point to a person who strikes your fancy, and say, "Go find me someone *gorgeous*. Really, really *gorgeous*." With a little luck, your herding dog will streak right to the person you're pointing to. Then say, "*Bring back* the cute one. *Bring back* the best looking person you can find!"

This trick is rather complicated and will take a lot of practice with your friends. But hey—maybe one of your friends might start looking pretty good, after all those practices with your dog fetching him or her. (It gives a whole new meaning to the phrase, "My, you look *fetching* today!")

Chivalry

Teach your dog to bring a rose to your favorite person.

The Skill: This trick requires a dog to hold an object, such as a rose with the thorns removed, and go to the person you indicate. (It could be a very serious faux pas—faux paw?—if your dog delivers the rose to the wrong person!)

How to Teach It: There are several ways to teach a dog to carry an object. Since this is trick training and just for fun, we'll assume your dog is something of a natural retriever and likes to carry things for you. (If he doesn't, simply pick another trick for him to do.) When he picks up a toy or other object, tell him "Good take it!" When he walks around with the toy in his mouth, say, "Good hold!" If he's a natural retriever, he'll quickly tune in to these cues.

The second part is to teach the dog to go to a person, which is explained in the Fetching From the Herd exercise above.

When the dog is reliable on both parts of the command, combine them. Give him a rose, and tell him to "take it" and "hold." Then point to the person you want to impress, and say, "Go to the *gorgeous* one—the *gorgeous* one!" With a little luck and skill, the dog will take the rose and actually deliver it to the gorgeous one—not the scary-looking person next to the object of your desire.

Rate a Guy or Girl

Do you want to shamelessly flatter someone? Ask your dog if he or she rates a 10!

> **The Skill:** This is a simple bark on command exercise. You say, "Wow, there's a hottie! What would you rate her (or him) on a scale of 1 to 10?" Then your dog barks 10 times. Shame on you if you're cruel to a human and only let your dog bark once or twice! You don't deserve your wonderful dog! It is acceptable to have the dog bark nine times—to which you can say, "Nine times? Oh that's right, you think there is no perfect 10."
>
> **How to Teach It:** Teach speak by saying, "Good speak" when the dog barks. Over time, the dog will bark for longer and longer periods. When he has barked the correct number of times (in this case, nine or 10), reward him with a treat. You can easily transfer this command to a hand signal. Hold your hand in a special way each time he's supposed to be barking, and he'll learn to bark when you hold your hand in that position, and stop barking when you end the hand signal.
>
> A warning: This is one trick in which you really want a barky dog. If he stops barking after just a few barks, he's just rated the person of your dreams as a three! This isn't going to impress anyone.

A Little Political Humor

The Only Good Republican (or Democrat)

You can use your dog to forward your political agenda. Ask your dog, "Would you rather be dead or be a Republican?" at which point he'll flop over dead!

The Skill: This is just a simple play dead exercise, but the dog flops over at the word "Republican" instead of "Play dead." Of course, use whatever word reflects your politics. You can have him play dead when you say, "Would you rather be dead or a Democrat" or "wear white after Labor Day" or "drink domestic beer." To the dog, it's just a trick!

How to Teach It: Your dog needs a reliable down-stay to learn this trick. While the dog is lying down, take a treat and move it along the ground, then up behind his elbow. This will position him so that he's lying on his side—at which point you say "Good Republican!" (or "Democrat" or "labor" or "beer"). Gradually have him hold the position for longer and longer periods of time before you give him a treat, so he seems to be "dead" for quite a while.

Icebreakers for Nice Dogs

You might prefer not to have your dog doing political humor—and may not be the kind of person who would have your dog rating people on a scale of one to 10 (and the thought that he might stop counting at three sends chills down your spine). You can still train your dog to do some easy tricks that will let him—and you—have more fun on your adventures!

Wag Your Tail

A wagging tail makes people feel welcome and happy. Your dog can learn to do it on command.

The Skill: Most dogs will wag their tails when you say their name. What could be easier than that?

How to Teach It: If you've got a tail-wagger, you don't really need to "teach" the command. Just say her name in a high-pitched, happy voice, and most dogs will start wagging their tails. Then you can say, "Lassie, are you glad to meet our new friend? Huh, Lassie? Lassie, do you like our friend?" Lassie will be wagging her tail because she likes to hear her name, but your friend will feel included and welcome. That's a good thing!

Wave

A wave from a dog is such a friendly greeting. This is also a great trick for shy dogs, because people stand back to see the dog wave.

> **The Skill:** At the command "wave," the dog paws up high in the air, and seems to wave to the crowd.
>
> **How to Teach It:** Hold a treat tightly in your hand; it's easiest if you hold your hand near the floor. The dog will be interested in the treat, and sooner or later will paw at your hand to get it. As soon as he paws, say "Good wave" and give him the treat. Soon, if you say "wave" and hold your hand in a fist, he'll paw at your fist. After he's become an enthusiastic pawer, tell him to sit and then hold your fist just a bit out of reach. He'll have to reach out with his paw—in what is a recognizable wave.

Shake Hands

It's always nice to shake hands in polite company.

> **The Skill:** This trick builds on the wave. Instead of waving into the air, the dog shakes hands.
>
> **How to Teach It:** Teach the wave, as I've just explained. When the dog is very sure of himself on the wave, reach out and gently take his paw, and say "Good shake." Give him a big treat right away, so he thinks shaking paws is fun.

Olo is a supremely polite dog.

Bow

A courtly dog will always bow when he meets a dignitary.

> **The Skill:** The dog puts his front legs on the ground and leaves his rear in the air, giving a formal doggie bow.
>
> **How to Teach It:** When the dog is standing, hold a treat between his front toes and then push it toward his rear. He'll have to "bow" down to get his treat.

The tricks you can teach your dog are endless. As you go into new situations, think about what tricks would be fun to do, and how to teach them. Also think about ways to make the trick funny—"playing dead" isn't funny, but your dog doing political satire might be.

It's a bonding, exhilarating experience to teach your dog tricks, and even more fun to share new adventures together. You'll both have a good time—and you'll make some people laugh, too.

Chapter 10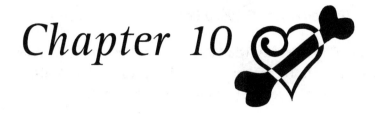

You Never Get a Second Chance to Make a First Impression (on the Dog)

Sometimes the shoe is on the other paw. You meet someone you'd like to get to know better when that person is walking her dog.

Even if you're not the type of guy this kind of woman usually dates, she might sit up and take notice if her dog likes you. Forget making a great first impression on the human—concentrate on making a great first impression on the dog. If you're the dog's type, the human may just come around.

That's exactly what Jed Allan did when he interviewed for the role of Scott Turner on the Lassie series in the 1960s, according to *TV Guide Online*. They report that Allan said:

> *Lassie was the star of the show, that was for sure. I met with the producers . . . then I had more meetings with other people. Later, I got a call saying that I had to have one more meeting.*
>
> *I asked, "Who else do I have to meet?"*
>
> *They said, "The dog."*
>
> *I thought they had to be kidding, but they said, "If Lassie doesn't like you, how can you work with him?" [Lassie was played by a male dog.]*
>
> *So I thought, how can I get this dog to like me? My wife . . . remembered that a . . . friend of ours . . . had a dog in heat. I went over, took my jacket off and rolled around in the dirt with his dog before my meeting with Lassie. When I met Lassie, [he] jumped up on me and started licking my face.*

How to Make Sure That Dog Adores You on Sight

Of course, this little ruse could have gone wrong in ways that are far too horrible to contemplate. There are a lot less risky ways to worm your way into a dog's heart.

Give the Dog a Treat

The way to a dog's heart is through his stomach. Have some yummy treats on hand. (It's best if they're all-natural, and of course ask permission before giving a dog a treat.) If you want a pooch to drag his human over to you every time you come in sight, just keep those treats coming!

Talk to the Dog Gently and Softly

Dogs hate it when people greet them loudly. Think about it: When do dogs speak loudly? When they're trying to get rid of an evil intruder. Bark! Bark!

When they see someone they love, dogs make little high-pitched, happy noises. If you do the same, dogs will love you.

Of course, at the same time dogs love sweet, high, happy voices, humans want to gag at baby-talk. You can make both the human and the dog happy by saying intelligent things in your high, happy voice. This will make you socially acceptable to the human and canine species.

 Carol and Chris: A True Love Story

Carol was representing her local dog training club at the Reno Sport and Boat show. Chris was at a different booth, representing the Nevada Division of Wildlife.

"Chris spotted my dog—a beautiful liver-spotted Dalmatian—and came across the very crowded convention center to see *her*," Carol remembers.

Chris wanted to get a dog, but told Carol he had allergies. "I recommended a Standard Poodle, not a Dalmatian," she says. Chris decided he was interested in Poodles—and in Carol. "A few months later, he called me and asked me to help him train his new Poodle puppy," says Carol. "Needless to say, we hit it off, and have been together ever since."

A year and a half later they were married, and 17 years after that first meeting, Carol says, "Chris now has six Dalmatians—and an obviously improved immune system."

While she is into showing as well as training, Chris loves the dogs but finds dog shows uninteresting. "He does take them for walks and on business trips and vacations," Carol says. "The dogs are very good ice breakers and open up conversations wherever we go."

Take a Lesson in Not-So-Heavy Petting

There's a great book called *The Other End of the Leash* by Patricia McConnell. One of the main premises of the book is that people are primates, and primates love to hug. Dogs are, well, dogs, and they hate hugging. The book contains hilarious pictures of people hugging their dogs while the human looks blissful and the dog has a look of enduring suffering.

Don't hug a dog. Don't whomp him on the side, yelling, "GOOD BOY! WHAT A GOOD BOY!" Don't approach with your hand over the dog's head (this is very rude in doggie language). Instead, stroke gently and quietly underneath the chin and on the chest.

The dog will like you. Equally important, that gentle, sweet, thoughtful interaction is a hint for your potential lover of just how considerate you can be.

Hmmmmm. . . .

Chapter 11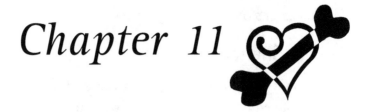

Where the Dogs Are

Remember the old movie *Where the Boys Are,* about college kids finding romance (and other things) on spring break? The boys all headed down to Fort Lauderdale because that's where the parties are . . . and the girls followed because, of course, that's *where the boys are.*

If you want to find romance with a dog lover, you just need to go *where the dogs are.*

America is full of dogs. In fact, there are about the same number of dogs in this country as there are kids under the age of 18. (For unknown and unjust reasons, we get no tax deduction for our four-footed family members—and we have to pay for their schooling; not a single politician is even suggesting vouchers. Go figure!)

Every weekend, there are vast congregations of canine enthusiasts having fun with their dogs. Check out these venues, and you'll find someone who shares your love of animals, and just might be a person who will want to share your future.

Animal Shelters

Every county in this country has a cadre of people who work endlessly to save homeless pets. If you want to meet some of the nicest people in the world, volunteer. It doesn't matter if you find going to the shelter depressing—there are plenty of jobs you can do off-site. Volunteer to write a newsletter, do their accounting, serve on a board of directors, solicit donations from local businesses, organize a fundraising bash—the homeless pets need all your talents.

For unfathomable reasons, almost all shelter volunteers are women. If you're a man who is truly looking for a caring, gentle soul who would be a great life partner, go to a shelter and look at the humans.

One small warning: Every volunteer who works at a shelter sooner or later adopts a dog whom absolutely no one in her right mind would adopt. And she finds it so rewarding that she adopts about four or five more. Consider this to be in your favor; she might be

You spend long hours together and share a vision of a humane world.
When two kind people volunteer together, you don't know what might happen.

Feel the Love

The Oregon Humane Society has a slogan: Feel the Love. You can bet when their pro-bono advertising agency thought up that motto, they were only thinking about the love between adopters and the dogs, cats, and other crea-

tures looking for their forever homes. But humane society staff and volunteers seem to have taken the motto at face value. You might have heard of people who are married to their work. Well, some of the volunteers were practically married at work. In fact, there are three marriages so far and counting at the Oregon Humane Society.

looking for a man who will look great with just a little cleaning up and some TLC. This woman is more likely to judge you by your heart than by your bank account.

Dog Shows

You've probably watched the famous Westminster Kennel Club dog show on television, and may have caught a few other shows if you're an Animal Planet fan. But did you know there are more than 1,400 all-breed dog shows held every year? Dog shows aren't just another activity—they're a whole subculture. These people are *serious* about their dogs.

Many of them drive to the show in trailers and RVs, with pictures of their top-winning dogs airbrushed on the side. The effort it takes to show a dog is incredible. These people are schlepping massive amounts of equipment: crates, exercise pens, hair dryers, food from home, water from home, a whole suitcase full of brushes and assorted

Famous First Lines

Dogs are great conversation starters. You don't need brilliant repartee to start talking with someone with a dog. In fact, corny lines work amazingly well with those of us who are besotted with our pooches. A woman who would rather spray you with pepper mace than hear one more trite come-on will listen for hours to the sweet nothings you whisper about her Weimaraner.

Here are a few memorable lines I have heard used to open a conversation.

 I'll never forget walking my dogs in downtown Portland when a man said, "In my next life, I want to be one of your dogs."

I smiled, but it's a line I hear all the time.

Then he paused, and said, "Wait, I bet you neuter your dogs, don't you?"

I admitted that I did.

He took another look at my happy pooches, smiled back at me at said, "Oh, it would be worth it."

 I have a friend with a big, unkempt-looking bear of a dog. When people say, "What is he?" my friend answers, "He's Jewish."

Sometimes my (Jewish) friend changes his answer and says, "He's Catholic."

 I have Papillons. They are tiny (about four to 10 pounds), with large, dramatic ears that look like butterfly wings.

leashes. Imagine how popular you could be if you just helped carry some of that heavy equipment. You would be a show exhibitor's dream date.

And even if you don't find the love of your life, there's nothing more entertaining than a dog show. The array of dogs is dizzying: Poodles

A gay friend saw them one day and said, "Ohmygod! They look just like cats in drag!"

A guy who obviously spent a lot of time in a gym was admiring a German Shorthaired Pointer—and the woman at the other end of the leash. Clearly trying to come up with the best compliment he could, the young man trailed his fingers lightly on the dog's rump and said, "Your dog looks like she works out—she's got great glutes."

A man looked at his friend's Basset Hound and asked, "Did you ever notice that your dog has a really cute butt?"

One friend says to every dog he sees, "This dog has such kind eyes." Judging by the smiles on the owner's faces, it works every time. And they start telling him about all the kind and loving things their dogs do.

A man with a very friendly dog says to every woman who pets the dog, "Wow, he really, really likes you. He thinks you're something special." Almost every time, the smiling, flattered woman stays longer to pet the dog—and get to know the friendly dog owner.

If the dog is long and leggy, and the owner is a woman—or if the dog is strong and buff, and the owner is a man, "Amazing. You and your dog really do look alike."

This line doesn't ever work—even if it's true—if the dog is a Bulldog, a Pug or a nervous little Chihuahua.

with their elaborate coifs in all shades of black, gray, blue, brown, café-au-lait, silver, apricot, cream and white. Naked Chinese Cresteds, kept warm in winter with sweaters and lovingly slathered with sun block (SPF 15 or higher) in summer. Massive Mastiffs with feet the size of dinner plates, and tiny Chihuahuas with paws the size of dimes.

When You Can't Think of Anything Clever

The moment finally arrives: There's a hottie at one end of the leash and a pooch who's compatible with yours at the other. And you can't think of anything remotely funny or clever.

Don't worry. Dog owners need only the tiniest excuse to start telling you about their dogs.

Anyone can come up with these opening lines, even if your pulse is racing, your palms are sweating, and you heart is beating so loudly it's hard to hear anything else.

- "What kind of dog is that?" This will start a conversation every time. If the dog's a purebred, the owner will launch into the history, attractiveness, loyalty and incredible intelligence of the breed. If the dog is a mix, the question can lead to hours of speculation about what combination of breeds could have created such an attractive, loyal and incredibly intelligent dog.

- If you know the breed, all you have to say is, "I love _____. Aren't they great dogs?" The owner will then spend an hour agreeing about just how great this dog is.

- When you can't think of anything nice to say about the breed, or the dog, all you have to say is, "Look at your dog." The owner will launch into a long description of the dog's virtues, just as if you'd said something coherent.

- If the cat got your tongue and you can barely croak a word in front of this amazingly attractive person and dog, all you have to do is say, "Awwwwwww. . . . " The owner won't notice for a second that you merely croaked a syllable. It's enough that you all agree this really is the most adorable dog in the whole world—which buys you plenty of time to think of a follow-up syllable.

And the humans are fun to watch, too, with their endless array of doggie-themed clothing. (A dog show may be the only place on earth to buy an *I ♥ My Otterhound* sweatshirt, not to mention a 14-karat gold Kuvasz charm bracelet.)

Doggie Day Care

Countless single parents have fallen in love at day care centers. Happily, meeting another concerned parent is no longer limited to people with human kids. Now there's doggie day care.

Ten years ago, doggie day care didn't exist. Apparently, dogs stayed home while the humans went to the office. Not anymore. Doggie day cares in some communities now outnumber the dog washes and dog training schools.

These places have become their own communities, with bonding among dogs—and among owners. Take, for example, Manhattan's Biscuits and Bath Doggy Village. This is a five-story doggie day care and gym, complete with a lap pool and play areas lined with Astroturf. Humans cater parties for their dogs, with gourmet treats for four-legged and two-legged guests.

If your dog has made a new best friend in doggie day care, it's only natural to ask the dog and owner out for a play date.

Doggie day care is pretty evenly divided between male and female humans, since good parents for their "fur kids" come in both genders.

Training Classes

Forget taking the community college course on Chinese cooking to meet a woman, or auto mechanics to meet a guy. Dog class is lots more fun—and the homework is easier.

From puppy kindergarten to tricks class to classes for problem dogs (like Growl Class for aggressive dogs)—you and your dog can take classes for years. And there's specialized training you'll want to take to get involved in doggie activities, like agility, obedience and herding. Life is good for the professional (canine) student!

 ## Liz and Paul: A True Love Story

It was the mid-1970s, and Liz was stationed with the military police at Naval Air Station Miramar in San Diego—along with a German Shepherd puppy named Max. "I grew up with my Mom's spoiled rotten Toy Poodles, and I was determined to have a well-trained dog," she says. She joined an obedience class. "Max and I trained often and we both enjoyed it."

One day she was out on the base training Max, and a young Marine walked by with his German Shepherd. He had his not-so-well trained dog off-leash, and as they walked past Liz and Max, his dog spotted a rabbit and took off, chasing the rabbit cross-country. Things got scary when the rabbit and dog headed for the runways of Miramar, where the jets take off and land.

The Marine called his dog, screaming at the top of his lungs, "Bullet, come! COME!" The dog totally ignored him. "As he chased his dog, I praised my dog for remaining with me, and shook my head over Bullet's lack of training," says Liz.

Luckily, dog and rabbit both survived the experience and no jets were harmed during the escapade. However, the Marine was chewed out royally by base officials for allowing his dog to run loose on base and potentially endangering aircraft.

"Several days later, he looked me up, asking how I had trained my dog. Paul and I were married a year and a half later," says Liz. The love affair between Liz and that young Marine—and their dogs—continues to this day. "I work as a professional writer and dog trainer, and we have competed with our dogs in agility, Schutzhund, herding, carting, obedience and Frisbee, and do therapy work. We just celebrated our 29th wedding anniversary and are still training dogs!"

The only drawback: The government hasn't made low-interest student loans available for canine training, and there isn't a single athletic scholarship at any dog school.

Sporting Events

If you're a woman seeking a dog-loving guy, look to local sporting events. Local baseball teams, especially minor league teams, frequently host "dog in the park" nights. Friendly dogs who aren't noise-sensitive might enjoy cheering for the home team, and meeting sports fans at the same time. You might enjoy it, too.

This brings us to a point to consider: Sometimes, just sometimes, humans can be too picky. I interviewed one woman who worked with a team of Frisbee dogs. Some of the biggest gigs on her schedule were baseball games.

"You know, you just never meet men in this job," she complained.

"Uh, didn't you just tell me that you were sitting in the dugout with the players?" I asked, incredulous.

"Well, yeah, but those guys are more like friends."

This woman is hanging out with professional athletes, and doesn't notice that her job has perks that most of ours don't! Of course, nowadays, you'd want to check with the parole officer of any player you meet. But still, her job sure beats working in the secretarial pool.

Dog Parks

Dog parks are the perfect place to sniff out new friends and begin to get frisky. And the dogs have a great time, too. This meeting place has become so ritualized that this activity has earned its own chapter. Turn the page to learn how you and your canine companion can find love unleashed at the park.

Chapter 12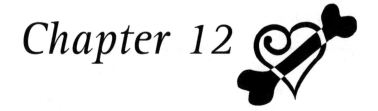

Energetic Dogs and Frisky Humans Getting Together and Having Fun

There was once a time when only hip New Yorkers had dog parks. Then they spread to trendy cities: San Francisco, Los Angeles, Chicago. Now they're everywhere—even small towns and the most conformist of suburbs.

Yes, the dog park is the new place to see and be seen. It replaces discos and bars, and is a much better place to meet people than a coffee joint (after all, you actually *talk* to people at the dog park).

Stacy and Bill: A True Love Story

Stacy will never forget the first day she took Jade for a walk in the park. She'd just adopted the German Shepherd the day before. It was a happy new adventure for them both to check out the park just around the corner from Stacy's Milwaukee, Wisconsin, home.

It was getting dark, and Jade was playing off-leash in a big field. "It was dusk and I couldn't see that well," Stacy says.

Suddenly, a Labrador Retriever appeared seemingly out of nowhere—and he was racing right toward Jade. Stacy held her breath, fearing there would be a fight. Instead, there was instant friendship. "They took off running together like they'd known each other their whole lives," she says.

A moment later, the Lab's owner came running through the dusk. "I didn't see your dog," he said. It turned out that Labrador Retriever MacGuyver and owner Bill Conroy lived just across the street from the park. Soon, Stacy, Bill, Jade and MacGuyver were walking their dogs together regularly. "Bill could see the park from his living room window, and he'd bring MacGuyver out when he saw us," says Stacy.

Stacy liked what she saw of Bill from the very first. "I could see how Bill loved and treated his dog—that was half the attraction."

After eight months of visiting at the park, Stacy and Bill had their first date. Marriage followed. This year, the couple welcomed a new member into their family—a baby boy named Aidan. Stacy says Jade and MacGuyver will help teach Aiden the compassion and kindness that still attracts her to Bill.

The Right Park

Just as you'll meet different people at a country-western bar than at a nightclub that features alternative music, you'll meet different people—and different dogs—depending on which dog park you go to.

Nowhere is this more true than in New York City, which boasts more than 30 fenced dog parks. "If you're looking for a specific type

Stacy looks back on the fateful day she adopted Jade and says everything in her life is different, and better, because of that decision. "I don't believe in coincidence," she says.

She's become very active in a group that's trying to establish dog parks in Milwaukee, and has a whole set of friends from that effort.

Stacy, Bill and all the family

Jade also led Stacy to a new profession. Jade was diagnosed with Addison's disease (a disorder that causes adrenal insufficiency), so Stacy started preparing wholesome, natural, homemade food for her dog. Soon other people wanted to buy the food for their dogs, and Companion Natural Pet Food was born. "First it took over the basement; now we have it manufactured," she says.

Stacy believes meeting over dogs is the perfect way to find the perfect mate. "You can see compassion in that person. You have an instant bond: You both love dogs."

For Stacy, adopting Jade has led to a lifelong love, a baby, friends and a new career. You never know what will happen when you take your dog for a walk in the park.

of guy or girl, you have to go to the right park," explains single Manhattan dog trainer and author of *Dog Friendly Dog Training*, Andrea Arden. "If you're looking for someone artsy and hip, go to Thompkins Square Park. Yuppies go to Madison Square Park." There's actually an amazing web site, www.urbanhound.com, that provides a complete guide for Manhattan dog lovers. This site rates all the dog parks, including comments on the surface, the size of the run, facilities (such as water and comfortable seating) and friendliness.

Smaller cities have fewer dog parks—and the people and dogs vary by time of day. "My favorite time is early on Sunday mornings," says Karen, who takes her dog, Edison, to one of only three dog parks in Portland, Oregon. "The people who are at the park on Sunday mornings are the type who used to get up early and go to church, before dogs became their religion." She says the Sunday morning dogs are the best behaved, and she won't even bring Edison on Saturday in the late afternoon, when the young guys with rowdy dogs take over the park.

Arden advises New York singles (or single city visitors) to go to Manhattan dog parks on weekends. "Generally, people who live in Manhattan and have relationships have a country home, where they go on weekends. The single people are usually in the city for the weekend."

Getting to Know You . . .

"The parks can be very cliquish," says Manhattan writer Nikki Moustaki. "If you're not in the clique, they might not even be nice to your dog."

Arden says these cliques can lead to love—but slowly. "You develop a little group of people; your dogs and theirs get along. So you all meet at a certain time. It starts as a platonic friendship, and may really expand over time," she says. "This is not a quick pick-up, it's a long-term relationship pick-up." Arden says people will usually see each other in the park at least five or six times before making a big romantic move. That gives you enough time to ask yourself the really important question: Do your dogs get along?

Dog Park Petiquette

There are definite do's and don'ts at the dog park. If you don't follow these codes of behavior (often unwritten), you'll find yourself getting the cold shoulder. You may even be asked to leave – depriving your pup of this slice of doggie heaven in an urban world.

✓ **No teeth!** The absolute code of the dog park is no aggression. This is supposed to be a fun time for humans and pooches alike. It isn't any fun for a dog if he's being harassed, annoyed or hurt by another dog. If you have a dog who is aggressive with other dogs (or humans), this isn't the place for him.

    If you have a rowdy dog, take the time to see how other people are reacting to him: Are they smiling at your happy, busy dog—or are they grimacing when your dog approaches theirs. What you may perceive as fun, other owners and their dogs might perceive as mugging. If you're not sure, talk with the other owners and ask if your dog's behavior is OK with their dog.

✓ **Scoop.** For the sake of hygiene, and to ensure that other owners can step wherever they please, clean up after your pet. Most dog parks are run by city and county governments, and fines can be hefty if you don't scoop up after your dog. Plus, you will be the least popular person in the park—and your pooch won't be far behind.

✓ **Spay or neuter.** There is a constantly changing cast of canine characters who have to sort out their relationships with each other. The dogs who are most likely to need to assert their dominance are intact dogs. If you spay and neuter, your dog will be calmer, and so will you.

✓ **Take responsibility.** If your dog hurts another dog (even in happy play), take responsibility. If you see a dog who needs help—even if your dog isn't involved—lend a hand. Most important, be there for your own dog. Check in with him often and make sure he's having a good time. Watch to see if he's thirsty, or if he's worried about another dog at the park.

Is My Dog Gay?

There is nothing more misunderstood in the world of dogs than humping. Unless a female is in heat and a male is mating with her, humping doesn't have a thing to do with sex.

Humping is a message to another dog that the dog on top is dominant. Whether the dogs are male or female is irrelevant. It's only our primate brains that interpret this as sex.

While some of this behavior is normal, too much means your dog is a bully.

✓ **Obey the rules.** Most dog parks are located in the middle of a "regular" park, where people come to jog, play with their children, get in a game of tennis, skateboard, sunbathe—and all the other things non-dog people do. Respect their needs. Leash your dog when you're out of the off-leash area. Don't give the other park users a reason to kick the dogs out.

Is Your Dog a Dog-Park Dog?

While dog parks are a fabulous place for many dogs, they're an ordeal for others. You need to decide if you have a dog-park dog. Here are some things to think about:

✗ **Dog parks are a bad place to socialize young puppies.** The dynamics of a dog park are incredibly complex—and they change hour by hour, as dogs come and go. Before you expose your puppy to this complex social dynamic, make sure he has social skills, learned by playing with other puppies and socially appropriate older dogs.

The day I wrote this chapter, I was at a dog park—and somebody brought a sweet four-month-old Border Collie mix.

Within five minutes, this poor pup had been bowled over by several of the more dominant dogs. He was sitting in a corner, tail tucked between his legs, avoiding eye contact with any other dog. This day, the puppy learned to fear other dogs. As he grows up, he's likely to either avoid other dogs or become a bully—putting other dogs in their place before they can frighten him.

✗ **Small dogs don't belong.** Even a friendly, lovable, big dog can step on your small dog and injure him. Even in the best of circumstances, squabbles happen at dog parks. If your dog weighs 10 pounds, he may not live through even a minor skirmish with a 100-pound dog.

You need to honestly evaluate how fragile your dog is. While a rugged little Terrier will probably be just fine at a dog park, a small, fine-boned Toy Poodle doesn't belong. Use your common sense to protect your dog.

Some cities have separate off-leash areas for small dogs—a great idea for the burgeoning number of small dogs in America.

Dog Park Alternatives

If you don't have a dog-park kind of dog, there are lots of alternatives. Here are a few.

Walk your dog some place chic. There are hip people hanging out in places other than dog parks. Take your dog on regular walks in the trendy part of town. Get to know the shopkeepers and neighborhood regulars. You and your dog will have fun, and you'll both benefit from the exercise.

Go to puppy kindergarten. Dog trainers will tell you this is the most important class they teach. Your dog will have the chance to play with other puppies as he learns basic obedience. After this confidence-builder, he might be ready for the complex social environment of the dog park.

Form a neighborhood play group. Get to know your neighbors who have nice dogs, and form a play group. You can meet in your yard, or rotate among the neighbors. You can pick and choose among the dogs who get along well—and have nice owners!

Start a breed play day. I have a (happily married) friend, Gail, who holds a Papillon play day at her home every month. Everyone who has a Papillon is welcome to come. These delicate little dogs can't play with big dogs—and they have such a great time when they run and wrestle with each other. My friend has had more than 30 Papillons at her house having the time of their lives. We consider Gail to be a goddess, and she says she loves having that much joy in her home every month.

People with Pugs are famous for great parties. I have friends who help organize a Schnauzer Walk (proceeds go to good causes). You don't have to go to the dog park to make friends.

Chapter 13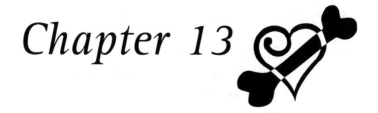

Whining and Dining With Dogs

When you think of dating, you probably envision going out to dinner. One of the hottest trends is going out to dinner with your dog. Believe it or not, in most states it's legal to dine with your dog, as long as the food is served outside.

This is a perfect summer activity—or a great activity in places that have sun all year long. Find that hip outdoor café, order your veggie burger and a steak, medium-rare, for your hound.

The Lucky Labrador Brew Pub

Cheers may have had the bar where everybody knows your name. Portland, Oregon has something better: the pub where everybody knows your dog's name. The Lucky Labrador Brew Pub caters to people and their dogs. Although the Lucky Lab offers inside dining (where Oregon health laws prohibit dogs), it's most famous for its outside tables. This part of the restaurant has 32 picnic tables—enough to seat about 200 people and their various dogs. And it's not unusual for the place to be packed.

Owner Gary Geist says it's a great place for singles to meet. "You bring a puppy in here and you get a lot of attention," says Geist. "The dogs are a conversation icebreaker. People love coming here and talking about each other's dogs."

Geist says it's worked out well for him to have a pub that caters to the doggie set. "A lot of places around town have signs in their outdoor areas that say NO DOGS. They don't want to offend any customer. But we approach this as our niche. We don't mind offending a few people, since we attract a lot of dog lovers."

Other pubs should take note. While even upscale bars can get too rowdy for comfort sometimes, the Lucky Lab is almost always a model of decorum, especially among the four-footed patrons. "We rarely have any problem among the dogs," Geist says.

The Lucky Lab opened a second pub across town. Careful not to upset the neighbors, the second pub opened up without a dog area. How did the neighborhood respond? The neighborhood association came to ask when doggie dining would be added. It seems some of the neighborhood association members were waiting to take their dogs to dinner.

While the Lucky Lab is one of the most famous doggie dining establishments, there are others. For example, Petswelcome.com reports that the Doggie Diner in Bellingham, Washington, welcomes dogs, and even has items on the menu for them. And Pepe's Café in Key West, Florida, provides toys, water bowls and snacks for pets.

Doggie Dining Petiquette

Restaurant owners don't have to let dogs eat in their outside areas. Be the kind of customer that any restaurant owner will want back. Here are some petiquette do's for dining al fresco with Fido:

Have a Cappuccino With Your Canine

Where the hip hang, you'll also find dogs.

No place is more hip than Starbucks—and it's turned into America's top hangout for dog lovers. In the Pacific Northwest (which now has Starbucks open 24 hours a day and Starbucks with drive-through windows), you'll almost always find people sipping their lattes while their dogs enjoy the attention of everyone walking past. Many Starbucks keep water bowls at their outside tables for dogs.

Aahhh, the good life! I wonder how many of the chocolate Labs who hang out at Starbucks are named Mocha?

Your dog should be well trained. Most outside cafes are on or next to sidewalks. If your dog is likely to growl or lunge at joggers, walkers, bicyclists or other dogs, he should have some obedience lessons before joining you for outside dining.

Pay attention to your dog. It can get hot on the sidewalk. Be sure your dog has plenty of water and is comfortable.

Be considerate of other diners. They really don't want your Poodle's face in their pasta or your Labrador lapping at their latte. Keep your dog in your space, and only let him approach strangers when they ask to pet your dog.

Good grooming counts. Mom was right. Bathe and brush your dog before going out.

Clean up after your dog. If you have a big dog who drools, *you* should clean up the spot, not the wait staff.

Keep your dog on a leash.

Tip extra! Remember, you want the servers to think doggie dining is a great idea.

Chapter 14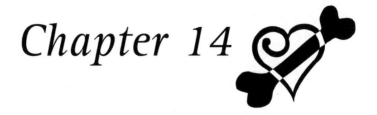

Turn-Offs and Do's and Don'ts

Glamour magazine has a Do's and Don'ts fashion section. Every woman in America is secretly afraid she'll open the magazine and see herself in the Don't section. The editors cleverly place a little black strip over the woman's eyes, supposedly disguising her identity. But they show the fashion blooper in toto—the bird legs sticking out of the big-legged pants, the bulges of fat under the too-tight top, the stringy hair under the flowery hat, the gigantic thighs in the miniskirt.

Still, maybe that little feature did some good. I know when I was a teenager, I'd take one last look at myself before I'd leave the door, just in case I was wearing something that might land my picture in the Don't section.

So here are some doggie dating do's, don'ts and turn-offs. Don't make me publish your picture!

Turn-Offs That Will Ensure You Never Meet a Dog Lover

1. **Violence.** *Duh*! (Oops! I find myself talking like a fashion magazine.) It shouldn't come as a shock that no dog lover will find you attractive if you're hitting your dog or yelling at her. But it's not just overt violence that's a turn-off. Jerking on the leash or calling the dog names like "dummy" are almost as icky. It's simple: Be kind to animals.

2. **Dirty dogs.** If your potential love interest pets your dog and comes away with a dirty hand, you won't get a second chance to make that first impression.

3. **Obese dogs.** This isn't about cosmetic attractiveness. It's about caring for your dog. An obese dog is one of the saddest sights there is, waddling along with none of the lightness and energy of a slender, healthy dog. I don't care if *you* have some extra pounds, but make sure your dog is slim, trim and looking her best.

4. **Ignored dogs.** Remember, part of what makes you attractive is the caring, loving relationship you have with your pet. If you get carried away with flirting and forget about your dog, you're likely to lose the object of your affection.

5. **Aggressive dogs.** If your dog is trying to hurt me or (worse yet) my dog, this isn't a love connection. Not every situation is appropriate for every dog. Make sure you bring your dog where he's comfortable, relaxed and doesn't act like he might hurt anyone else.

6. **Out-of-control dogs.** If you find yourself saying, "Don't worry, he's friendly!"—you're the only person who isn't rolling their eyes and hating your dog. In public places your dog belongs on a leash and shouldn't be mugging people or other dogs. Period.

Bad Touching

When you were a child, you were probably warned about "bad touching." If someone touches you someplace that feels uncomfortable, run away and tell an adult!

If your family member was guilty of "bad touching," you'd probably be the first person to suggest he should be carted off to jail. Unless the bad toucher is your dog. Then you probably think it's cute. Here's a news bulletin: No one else is amused. If your dog puts his nose to my private parts, I don't think it's funny. And it's less funny when he leaves a wet mark.

And I don't want to be humped on a first date by a man or his dog. Bad touching rules don't just apply to humans; they apply to dogs as well. While a polite sniff to another doggie butt is entirely socially acceptable, it's no fun for the dog who is the sniffee to have his personal areas rooted around in by a pushy nose. Dogs have their personal spaces, too. And getting humped by another dog is often an invitation to a fight.

Remember the motto "Just say no" when your dog is acting like a jerk.

7. **Not using a pooper-scooper.** Would you be attracted to someone with such a lack of hygiene—not to mention disregard for other people?

8. **Driving your pick-up with the dog in back.**

What's in a Name?

You know the line from *Romeo and Juliet*, protesting that a name doesn't count:

> *What's in a name? That which we call a rose by any*
> *other name would smell as sweet.*

Don't take Shakespeare's advice when you name your dog. Your social life just might balance on your dog's name. And dog names are the window to the soul of other dog owners.

People to Avoid—Even if the Dog Is Cute

Names can give a clue to the character of the owner. Avoid anyone who does the following:

- ✗ **Names a dog after a weapon.** Kind-hearted people hardly ever name their dogs after firearms. Run, don't walk, to the self-help section of your local bookstore if you find yourself attracted to a man with two Dobermans named Smith and Wesson or a Rottweiler named Luger.

- ✗ **Names a dog after an alcoholic beverage.** You might want to hold off dating a woman with dogs named Chardonnay, Chablis and Merlot until she decides to name one Recovery.

- ✗ **Names a dog after an ex-spouse.** A man who names his dog after his ex-wife so he can say, "Judy, I told you to shut up and sit," may not be your ideal mate.

- ✗ **Gives a dog an embarrassing name.** For example, the woman who names her male dog Precious and paints his nails may be too deranged for a long-term relationship.

- ✓ **Well, sometimes an embarrassing name is OK.** Jim Whitaker, the mayor of North Platte, Nebraska, promised "to walk naked" for a good cause. Soon, the little town was fielding phone calls from all over the world, asking about the mayor's proposed obscene exposure. You guessed it: Naked was the name of a little Poodle mix who accompanied Whitaker on a fund-raising walk for the North Platte Humane Society. The mayor's stunt got so such attention that the humane society almost doubled its expected amounts of contributions. In this instance, the mayor is forgiven for calling the little dog an embarrassing name.

Consider This When You Name Your Dog

🐕 **Everyone will call you by your dog's name.** Of the millions of people who see each other on their daily dog walks, painfully few remember the names of any other human. All of them know the names of the dogs. When John is walking Fuzzbutt and Susie is taking Furface for a stroll, they don't greet each other with "Hi, John" and "Good morning, Susie." It's always, "Hey there, Fuzzbutt, how are you doing boy?" and "You look great today, Furface." Consider noble, alluring names that will make you sound wonderful: Prince, Colossus, Adonis, Elle, Grace, Bright Eyes.

🐕 **Don't give your dog the same name as a person you're likely to date.** Do you think you might ever want to spend an intimate moment with someone named Kevin, Kathy, Chloe or Charles? Then it's a really poor idea to give your dog one of those names. Don't ever use a name for a dog that you might later want to say with passion. I once had a coworker who was wild about his Shetland Sheepdog named Shelley. That was fine, until he got a secretary named Shelley. The woman didn't find the confusion the least bit amusing.

When Seemingly Sane People Go Way Too Far

Not all the strange ideas in this book are mine. Many of them come from my friends. This is how writers make their living.

But sometimes you have to worry about your friends. Believe it or not, there were some ideas that my friends suggested that I rejected. These measures were even too desperate for me.

Take the following—*please.*

Kidnapping

I swear that my nephew seems pretty normal. Well, okay, he shaves his head. And we won't even talk about his tattoos. But when I had this discussion with him—well, you can imagine my fervent belief that he must take after his mother's side of the family.

> Unnamed Nephew: *Cool. A book on dogs as date bait. I can dig it.*
>
> Prominent Dog Writer: *So, you're 20 years old and single. Any great ideas?*
>
> Unnamed Nephew: *Pit bulls, dude.*
>
> Prominent Dog Writer: *Actually, women usually go for a softer, sweeter dog. Think about a Golden Retriever. Or a Sheltie.*
>
> Unnamed Nephew: *No, dude. You get a Pit Bull, and force the girl into a car.*
>
> Prominent Dog Writer: *Uh, you frighten me.*

Kinda Pedophile Weird

If you think my 20-year-old nephew is weird, wait until you hear what one middle-aged dog trainer I know said. I swear I'm not this making up. This woman was married—and just wanted to give me ideas to help all those unfortunate single people.

> Unnamed Normal-Looking Dog Trainer: *So, you could cover your dog in catsup, and yell, "Help me! Help me! My dog's just been hit by a car!"*
>
> Prominent Dog Writer: *But that's sick. And don't you think the person you just fooled will be really, really angry at you as soon as he figured out what you'd just done to him?*
>
> Unnamed Normal-Looking Dog Trainer: *Oh, right. So, how about you come to the park, with just a leash, in tears, saying your dog ran away? You wouldn't even have to own a dog!*

Prominent Dog Writer: *Uh, same problem. I think you're sounding desperate. Really weird and desperate.*

Unnamed Normal-Looking Dog Trainer: *Well, how about just going to a group of people and saying that there's a lost puppy in the area, and that you're looking for it, and want them to come help you?*

Prominent Dog Writer: *Yikes! That's the exact technique they warn kids that pedophiles use! You're even scarier than my nephew.*

Chapter 15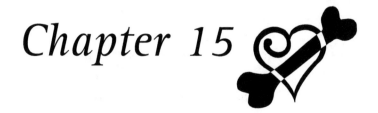

15 Activities You Can Do With Your Dog That Are Guaranteed to Bring You New Friends (and Maybe Even Romance)

It's easy to feel discouraged when you are a single person. It seems that all our friends get married in huge mating frenzies—and we're the only ones left behind.

Whether you've been single your entire life, or just recently left a relationship, it can be hard to find entertaining things to do on your own. Admit it: Even the most independent among us sometimes find ourselves whining like a bored, bored, bored kid during summer vacation . . . *But there's nothing fun to do!*

Happily, if you have a dog, there's *always* something to do (in addition to vacuuming up fur). The world is full of organized dog activities. I promise that every one of these activities can become the focal point of every minute of free time you have. And chances are you'll find at least one of the them completely, totally, fabulously entertaining for both you and your dog.

A plus: Organized dog activities are usually very social. Dog people, like their pets, seem to enjoy running in packs. These activities are definitely places to meet friends for a lifetime—and possibly the love of a lifetime.

Some of these activities—such as agility and obedience events—require practice before you're ready to compete. But while your dog is in training, local clubs and event organizers are begging for help putting up equipment and organizing the event records. There's always a place for a friendly newcomer.

Here are 15 activities to think about. Try at least one or two that might suit you and your dog. I promise you'll have a blast! And all of these activities enable you to get out, meet new people, explore new things—with your dog at your side. What could be better than that?

Canine Sporting Events

There is a sport for every human and every dog. It doesn't matter if you're young or old, buff or out of shape. You can have a mixed breed, or a highly specialized hunter or herder. You can aim for national titles, or be happy just to enjoy the activities with your friends.

Agility

Enthusiasts say agility is as much fun as a dog can have with his fur on. Dogs race through an obstacle course—careening over A-frames, dashing through above-ground tunnels, flying over hurdles—and generally having the time of their lives.

Agility classes are taught in every city in America, and it is now the nation's fastest-growing dog sport. Although the top competitors are true athletes (the dogs and the humans), beginning agility is great for almost every dog, and for every person, regardless of size, shape or age.

Sponsoring organizations include the American Kennel Club (purebreds only), and the United Kennel Club (UKC), North American Dog Agility Council (NADAC) and United States Dog Agility Association (USDAA)—which all welcome mixed breeds. Check these organizations out, and go to an agility trial in your area. There, you'll meet lots of friendly people who can tell you where to find a local trainer and get involved.

For Information

While the AKC only allows purebreds to enter its competitions, you can participate with your unregistered (spayed or neutered) purebred dog. This is great news, especially for people who enjoy AKC events and got their dog from a rescue organization. Check out the information about the AKC Indefinite Listing Privilege to learn how to participate with your purebred, spayed or neutered, unregistered dog. The AKC has a fabulous web site on all things relating to purebred dogs (including their agility events) at www.akc.org.

Purebreds and mixed breeds are both welcome at USDAA events. Go to www.usdaa.com for information.

Like the USDAA, NADAC welcomes mixed breed dogs. Check them out at www.nadac.com.

The UKC has a wide variety of performance events, including agility and obedience, and welcomes spayed and neutered mixed breeds to compete through their Limited Privilege Listing. Go to www.ukcdogs.com for information.

Jack and Angela: A True Love Story

There wasn't much in the world of dogs and dog training that Jack Moore hadn't done when he retired to the small central Oregon town of Sun River. He was something of a legend in the world of canine sports: He'd had top obedience, tracking, conformation and Schutzhund (protection training) dogs. And he'd done it with some of the most improbable breeds, including Bull Terriers and Airedales. So when Jack moved to Sun River, the first thing he looked for was some dog training buddies. "I talked with the veterinarian and asked him who trains dogs. I went to a newcomers' party and asked people there where to go for dog training."

Everyone answered with one word: Angela.

There was just one little problem—Angela didn't teach classes. And she didn't really want to. "I helped people sometimes who came to me with problems. I told them not to tell anyone, but this was a small town and they told people." She had run a couple of classes (and then gave her profits to Guide Dogs for the Blind), but she had no intention of teaching another class. "When Jack came to me, I gave him my standard line: I don't teach classes," says Angela with a laugh. But she soon realized

Angela and Jack visit with a friend's Border Terrier puppy

that Jack was an expert at something she wanted to know more about: tracking. He'd trained dogs to follow the scent of a human. "I told him I'd like to learn. We met in a park, and he started showing me."

They began to practice with their dogs more and more together, especially tracking. They'd go out and lay a track, walking the route the dog was to follow, sometimes sprinkling pieces of hot dog over the course so the dog understood he was supposed to follow his nose. Then they'd wait a couple of hours before taking the dog on the track, passing the time by sipping tea, talking, becoming friends, sharing stories.

"Once, we looked and there was a coyote eating the hot dogs!" says Angela. They later took the dogs out, and the dogs tracked the trail as if the coyote had never been there.

After all the hours together, friendship blossomed into romance. "Neither one of us was looking for romance, so we weren't trying to impress each other. We found we had more in common than just dogs," says Jack. Then he pauses, chuckles, and says, "And one thing just led to another." Angela agrees that the stress-free time of hanging out with dogs gave them a basis for the relationship. "We weren't really dating. We were just getting together with our dogs."

For the past 18 years, the two have continued in their love of dogs, and of each other. Jack has since had several hip surgeries and is mostly retired from dog sports. But not before he showed a whole new generation in a whole new sport just what's possible. Agility was just becoming popular, and a friend told Jack that he could train his Airedale, Casey, to do the obstacle course with just voice commands.

And that's exactly what he did. No longer able to run, Jack would stand in the center of the ring, calling out to Casey to go left or right, to jump, and weave and climb. This master trainer, and the dog who loved him, were so closely bonded that the dog listened and ran through those courses with all his heart. "The whole place would get quiet. The performance in the other ring would actually stop, because the judges wanted to see Jack and Casey. A lot of us were in tears," says Angela.

Casey retired at age 12, and Jack is in his 80s, but you can't go to an agility trial in Oregon without hearing the story of those two. They changed how people in this part of the country view the sport.

Angela has a new dance partner nowadays, but Jack isn't jealous. She's started to get involved in the sport of canine freestyle—dancing with dogs. And she won top honors at the first trials she entered.

Jack and Angela are grateful that their dogs brought them together, and are still clearly in love. Their advice: Do things with your dog and you never know what might happen. Says Angela, "If you're out doing dog activities, you may find someone else with the same passion."

A Jack Russell Terrier takes on the tire jump. You may or may not find the human love of your life at an agility trial, but you're guaranteed to have a great time with your dog!

Obedience Competition

If you stopped training your dog at puppy kindergarten, you might be surprised at how much you missed. Advanced obedience dogs work on hand signals, retrieve dumbbells over a high jump and find items just by scent. All of the dogs from a class line up and do a three-minute-long sit and a five-minute-long down—while their owners leave the building.

If you were turned off by old-fashioned training methods (and who wasn't?), where owners jerked on their dogs' leashes and demanded the dog perform *or else*—take heart. Modern obedience training is fun for dog and owner. The dog gets praise and a treat for doing his work right, and the owner gets to enjoy a happy dog with a merrily wagging tail.

For Information

The two largest sponsoring organizations are the AKC and UKC. Dogs must be purebred to compete in the AKC, but spayed and neutered mixed breeds are welcome at UKC events.

Rally Obedience

This newly emerging sport is a hybrid between agility and obedience. Dogs and their handlers negotiate a timed gymkhana course while heeling. It includes amazing turns, spins and serpentines that sometimes leave the handler a little dizzy, and the dog wagging her tail. Rally-O is a fun introduction to obedience, and is a great alternative to agility for dogs who don't have the right structure for all the running, jumping and pounding of the agility course.

For Information
At the time of this writing, Rally-O is a nonregular (just for fun—no titles) class with the AKC, but may eventually become a competitive sport. For information, go to www.akc.org.

Dancing With Dogs

Has it been a long time since someone asked you to go out dancing? Well, how about asking your dog to dance with you? Dancing with dogs—officially called canine musical freestyle—combines obedience, tricks and movements of the dog and handler, and sets them to music to form a dance routine. You pick your music, from a dignified waltz to hip hop, and you get to wear a cool costume (your dog can wear a matching collar). Because you pick your own music and routine, this sport is equally accessible no matter what shape, size, age and mix you and your dog happen to be. So dance, dance, dance!

For Information
Go to the World Canine Freestyle Organization's web site at www.worldcaninefreestyle.org.

Field Trials

While some of us like to dance with our dogs, traditionalists might rather hunt with them. Activities range from local hunters getting together to big-time professionals in national competitions for the best gun dog.

For Information

You can learn about clubs and events by going to the Dogs Unlimited web site (www.dogsunlimited.com) and clicking on "Out in the Field." You can also find more information at the AKC web site.

Frisbee

If you'd rather have your dog catch flying discs than hunt flying birds, there's a place for you in Frisbee competition. What starts out as simply throwing a pie tin–shaped toy for your dog can quickly evolve into incredible aerial moves above the ground.

It's a great event to watch, and if you have an athletic, nimble dog, it can be the Ultimate Dog Sport – if that's what you're looking for.

For Information

Go to the Dogpatch web site (www.dogpatch.org), and click on "Frisbee." You'll get a slew of links on training, organizations, rules and upcoming events.

Dog Shows

You've probably watched a dog show on TV, and might even have gone to see one. How about joining the sport and showing your dog?

Show dogs must be registered with the AKC. (There are also smaller shows, organized by other kennel clubs, including the United Kennel Club and the American Rare Breed Association.) Because dog shows are considered an evaluation of breeding stock, show dogs aren't spayed or neutered.

Judges do not really compare the dogs to one another. Rather, they select the dog that most closely conforms to its breed standard—a blueprint that describes the height, weight, color, head, tail and even toes of the ideal dog of your breed.

To get started, go to some shows and watch your breed in the ring. Meet the exhibitors, and find out why certain dogs are considered tops in their field.

What if your pooch isn't a show prospect? Do something else fun with your dog. After all, your dog will always be best in show in your heart.

For Information
Go the AKC web site and check out "A Beginner's Guide to Dog Shows."

Earthdog Events

If you have a Dachshund or terrier, that little guy is probably digging up your yard. Why not focus this tenacious energy into the sport of earthdog? In this sport, dogs go through elaborate underground mazes to find a rat at the end of the tunnel. (Don't worry if you're a rodent-lover. The rodents at earthdog tests are kept safe and secure in wire cages that are placed behind metal bars. The dogs, however, think the hunt is the real deal.)

Admittedly, earthdog enthusiasts have to do more work than the dogs in this sport. Volunteers construct elaborate tunnels (made of wood for safety), complete with turns, wrong exits and plastic "roots" that dogs have to squeeze past on their way to the caged rats. So the event can simulate natural hunting conditions, the tunnels are buried underground. "Rat tea," an aromatic concoction of used nesting materials mixed with water, is sprayed at the entrance to the tunnel and at strategic places along the interior, giving the dogs a scent trail to the rats.

Dogs must be purebred terriers or Dachshunds.

For Information
Earthdog tests are sanctioned by the American Kennel Club (www.akc.org).

Sledding

If you think sled dog races are just for people who live in Alaska (or maybe Minnesota), think again. There's sledding activity in almost every state, including (of all places) Arizona. In the mild Pacific Northwest, some determined mushers have competitions on wheeled sleds along the Oregon coast.

So check out the sport and get going. As the mushers say when they're telling their dogs to get started, *"Hike!"*

For Information
You can find links to sledding clubs and events at Sled Dog Central, www.sleddogcentral.com.

Flyball

This is a noisy, incredibly fast, fun doggie relay race. Dogs compete in teams of four. The first dog on each team flies over four low hurdles, smacks a device that then pops up a tennis ball, catches the ball in his mouth, and races back over the hurdles. As soon as one dog finishes, the next dog on the team starts. Two teams race side-by-side; the relay team with the fastest time progresses on to the next round of competition.

If you have a tiny dog, this might be the sport for you. The hurdle heights are lowered for teams with a small dog, so flyball enthusiasts are always looking for a fast little guy—called their "height dog."

For Information
Check out this incredibly fast-paced sport at the North American Flyball Association web site, www.flyball.org.

Weight Pulls

While some dogs are built for speed, others are built for strength. Lots of brawny dogs enjoy pulling weights. Some competitions are done with sleds on snow; others are done with wheeled carts. The handlers are never, ever allowed to touch or force the dog, so all weight pulling is voluntary.

Many of the competitions are divided by weight classes, so if you have a 40-pound dog, he'll be judged against other dogs in his category—and not against a 140-pound Mastiff.

For Information

To learn more about pulling events for Nordic (sledding) breeds, go to Sled Dog Central (www.sleddogcentral.com). The International Weight Pull Association has weight pulls that are open to all breeds, including mixes. Find them at www.eskimo.com/~samoyed/iwpa. The United Kennel Club also sanctions weight pulls. Look them up at www.ukcdogs.com.

Herding

In the old days, people got Border Collies (and other herding dogs) to tend their sheep. Nowadays, people get sheep to keep their Border Collies amused. There are clubs and events that bring people who love their herding together. The activities range from herding instinct tests (which any breed or mix can sometimes take), which require no training, to incredible tests of skill and endurance for seasoned herding dogs.

For Information

Go to the incredible Dogpatch web site (www.dogpatch.org) and click on "Herding" for information, links and events.

Lure Coursing

Do you have a leggy sighthound who is built for speed? Some dogs are born to run, and lure coursing is just what nature intended them to do. Sighthounds of all kinds—including big dogs like Borzoi, compact Basenjis and even diminutive Italian Greyhounds—compete for

Here Boy! Here Girl!

When it comes to canine activities, not everything is created equal, gender-wise. Men and women compete equally at all canine sports and activities; none of them have exclusively men's or women's competitions, like golf or tennis do. However, some activities attract mostly women and some attract mostly men. If you're looking for a woman, check out agility, obedience or dancing with dogs. Although there are certainly men at these events, women outnumber them at least five-to-one. And if you're looking for a man, try field trials, weight pulls, sledding, and Frisbee.

Of course, love can happen anywhere. If you're participating in an activity that you and your dog love, that's always a good thing. And if you just happen to meet a human partner who shares your passion for the sport—while you share your passion for each other—that can be as good as it gets.

titles as they chase a lure around a track. (If you're a rabbit lover, don't worry. These dogs are chasing plastic bags, not bunnies.)

This activity is especially wonderful for retired racing Greyhounds, who have the joy of life with a family—and still get to flash across a track every once in awhile like they did in their racing glory days.

For Information
The American Kennel Club sanctions lure coursing events. See details at www.akc.org.

When You and Your Dog Make a Difference

While you're thinking of cool things to do with your dog—where you'll just happen to meet tons of people—consider activities that make a meaningful difference.

These aren't just hobbies or sports; they take the human-animal bond to a whole new level. In these humanitarian pursuits, your dog is the senior partner and you take some life lessons from him.

Search and Rescue

These canine heroes have a nose for lost souls—whether it's finding a missing child or combing through the rubble after an earthquake or terrorist attack.

Dogs who respond to cataclysmic events in cities—such as the events of September 11, 2001—are urban search and rescue dogs. These highly trained dogs are certified by the Federal Emergency Management Agency (FEMA). Although some of these dogs are handled by highly skilled volunteers, most are handled by search and rescue professionals.

However, area search dogs are almost always handled by volunteers—and you and your dog might be suited to join the dedicated men and women who spend their free time helping others. When a child wanders off or hikers are lost in the woods, law enforcement officials often call in these highly trained and certified volunteers and their dogs to search for the missing person. These dogs can cover five times the area of a human, and are more accurate when they do.

Occasionally, dogs and handlers who start out as area search dogs qualify for more training, and become part of the FEMA task forces that tackle urban search and rescue.

For Information

To learn more about search and rescue, go to the National Association for Search and Rescue web site, www.nasar.org, and click on "SAR Dogs." For a list of more than 400 search and rescue units—including some that might be looking for volunteers, go to www.nasar.org/webdata/searchresource.shtml. You can find more information about urban search and rescue dogs at the Federal Emergency Management Agency web site, www.fema.gov. Click on "Urban Search and Rescue" and then "Canines."

Animal-Assisted Therapy

Therapy dogs visit everyone from people with mental illness to kids who are learning to read to senior citizens and hospice patients. These dogs listen, snuggle and sometimes even help with physical therapy.

Just as not every human is cut out to be a social worker, not every dog is going to be happy as a therapy dog. But if you have a friendly dog who loves being touched and held by people, and if you are willing to spend the time and attention to train him and to condition him that strange noises, sights, and equipment are all good—you two might be a great therapy team.

Many communities have local groups that provide support and training for people who are interested in doing animal-assisted therapy. You can learn about local affiliates to the two largest organizations (Delta Society and Therapy Dogs International) through their web sites. You might also check with your local humane society to see if there are other local therapy groups in your community.

For Information

The largest therapy animal organizations are the Delta Society (go to their web site at www.deltasociety.org, and click on "Pet Partners") and Therapy Dogs International (www.tdi-dog.org).

Chapter 16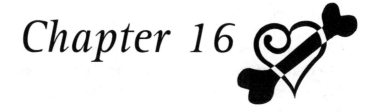

Single Buff Puppy . . .

SINGLE BLACK FEMALE . . . Seeks male companion-
ship, ethnicity unimportant. I'm a very good looking girl
who LOVES to play. I love long walks in the woods, rid-
ing in your pickup truck, hunting, camping and fishing
trips, cozy winter nights lying by the fire. Candlelight
dinners will have me eating out of your hand. Rub me
the right way and watch me respond. I'll be at the front
door when you get home from work, wearing only what
nature gave me. Kiss me and I'm yours. Call 555-1212
and ask for Daisy.

An Internet legend has it that this ad ran in the *Atlanta Journal-Constitution* and prompted more than 15,000 replies. The men who responded, the story goes, found themselves talking to the local Humane Society about an eight-week-old black Labrador Retriever.

What this story claimed worked for Daisy the puppy can work for humans, as well. Sometimes it pays to advertise.

Let's face it, there's a good chance we aren't going to meet our mate in the course of our everyday activities. Personal ads can sometimes bring interesting people into our lives. And sometimes, those people are even interesting in a *good* way!

Testing My Theory

Here's my theory: Ads that focus on dogs should produce better results than run-of-the-mill ads that only mention pets in passing. The concept is that the positive feelings people have for us when we're with our dogs will also be elicited by our ads.

I decided to do an actual experiment to test this theory. The person writing the ad would have one ad that was very doggie and one that wasn't. If I was right, the doggie ads would attract more people, and those people would be kinder, more compassionate people.

Now I just needed some experimental laboratory people to test the hypothesis.

I was eventually able to coerce some friends into letting me run personal ads for them in a local weekly paper, on the condition that I didn't use their real names. (It's important for aspiring dog writers to have a lot of friends. You need them. Writers and their friends make a lot of sacrifices in the name of science!)

The Ads

Justine (not her real name) is a teacher who competes in dog shows with her Golden Retrievers. She decided her doggie ad would describe her dog Polo (not his real name either), rather than herself. She hoped to find a guy who suited her as well as her dog. Here's Justine's doggie ad:

> *Golden Opportunity*
> *Looking for outdoorsy, faithful, true, hard-working,*
> *snuggling teddy bear kind of guy, who loves water sports.*

Lisa and Hilayne: A True Love Story

Dogs and the Internet can add up to love. Just ask Lisa. "My partner and I met online in a women's chat room. You put in a little profile of yourself when you join the chat room, and I mentioned my dogs in mine."

She got a reply from Hilayne, who was a dog lover, too. "We started talking about dogs and dogs showing: She had Poodles, lived in Massachusetts and had retired from showing her dogs; I had Akitas and Cardigan Welsh Corgis, lived in Maine and was showing actively."

When Lisa drove her dogs to a show in Springfield, she and Hilayne decided to meet. "After that, we would meet as often as we could while I was on my way to shows."

After about eight months of seeing each other on trips, Hilayne moved to Maine, and then the couple moved to Rhode Island together.

"Hilayne has gotten back into Poodles and she has converted me to a Poodle person," says Lisa. Eight years later, the couple owns eight Poodles, and are on the road showing together. Lisa's a dog photographer and writer. She says proudly, "All of this because of our dogs."

Blonde hair, brown eyes a plus. I'm tall, 36, SWF, professional.

For her not-so-doggie ad, Justine gave her own particulars:

Outgoing SWF 36 teacher, likes country music, camping, volunteering for good causes. Seeking nice, tall guy who likes animals. Light or non-drinker.

Ella is a 22-year-old artist and vegan. She recently talked a bank into giving her a line of credit that equals half her annual salary, so that she could pay for total hip replacement for her Pit Bull, Brad (get it . . . Brad Pit!). This woman has a great relationship with her gentle, sweet dog, but she hasn't been so lucky in love with two-footed guys. In fact, compared to some of her relationships, Brad, bad hips and all, has been a real bargain.

Her doggie ad was a description of Brad:

> *Looking for Mr. Nice*
>
> *You are: unique, loving, goofy, full of energy and spunk, sweet as a lamb. I am: 22, have a large dog and I love him.*

And her not-so-doggie ad:

> *22 SWF, a bit unconventional, enjoys nature, likes to DO things—no TV watching. I don't harass animals or eat them.*

Karen is a successful manager in a large corporation (Karen is the name this woman always gives in bars to men she wants to avoid). She's a mom to a teenage son and a mixed-breed dog, Edison, who was adopted from the local humane society. She decided to write her doggie ad in a way that might attract another dog lover and would suggest a non-threatening first date.

> *Just a Walk in the Park*
>
> *Energetic, smart, friendly, outgoing, youthful, fun-loving, big smile, fit, short—that's my dog. We want a walking partner. Are you—and maybe your dog—compatible?*
> *Boomer female looking for man's best friend's best friend.*

And Karen's not-so-doggie ad:

> *Funny, acerbic, SF boomer—world traveler, gardener, reader, walker, mom and animal-lover. Seeking smart, nice, outgoing guy. Must share well.*

Doggie Dating On-Line

On-line personals, including Match.com, have been wildly success-ful. More than ever before, singles are hooking up on-line.

There have been a few personal ad sites for animal lovers. So far, they haven't caught on enough to provide the volume of people nec-essary to be effective.

The best bet for finding love on-line: go to a major site but write a dog-friendly ad.

Delilah is a professional pet writer with three Papillons. (This dis-guise may not be doing too well.) Anyway, she figured that since she was paying for ads for her friends for her book, she should have a chance to find love, too. She hesitated to admit her age (50) in the ad, until a friend told her that "50 is the new 40." She just hopes the men reading her ad know that, too. Delilah's doggie ad:

Everything You Need to Know

Everything you need to know you can learn from your dog. Going for a ride is great. Coming home is great. Mornings are great. Nights are great. Give your loved one wet kisses when she comes home. SWF 50 seeking man who has learned this wisdom.

Delilah's not-so-doggie ad:

Brainy and funny writer, independent spirit, animal-lover, SWF 50. Seeks man who is smart, compassionate, happy with his world—to share conversations, adven-tures, Portland.

The Results

Here are the results of this experiment:

1. The 22-year old got twice as many responses as the older women. So much for "50 being the new 40;" evidently 50 will never be the new 20. Sigh!

2. The doggie ads attracted twice as many responses as the non-doggie ads. The major comment made by men responding to these ads was that they liked dogs, too. Several suggested meeting to walk dogs and get to know each other.

3. While a few of the responders sounded suspiciously like they were taking mind-altering substances and had no discernable means of support, many were nice guys. They included teachers, firefighters, artists and business executives. Each person placing an ad got at least one response that she seriously considered following up.

4. The most successful ad was Ella's "Looking for Mr. Nice." Interestingly, the least successful was Justine's "Golden Opportunity." Since both of these ads were written describing the subject's dog, the difference is puzzling. The only conclusion we could draw was that it's easier for men to identify themselves as "goofy and sweet as a lamb" than "faithful, true and hard-working."

5. Ella's ad that said she had a large male dog drew a number of men who said they had large female dogs who needed a nice playmate. So (neutered) Brad Pit just might find his canine equivalent of Jennifer Anniston, while Ella might find love at the other end of the leash.

6. The examples used in the chapter were all women simply because those were the only people I could wheedle, cajole and intimidate into placing ads. Doggie classifieds work just as well for men as for women. How do we know? In the same newspaper that contained our experimental classifieds, a man

wrote an ad with the headline "Just Like a Dog Only Better"
At least one of my hardy band of classified writers has
decided to give this guy a call.

Writing a Successful Personal Ad

Here are some tips for writing the perfect ad:

✓ **Be careful what you say.** With all the on-line personals, as
well as those in community papers, the "want ads" are a place
to find nice people. They're also a place to find very strange
people. Be careful of words that will attract the truly weird.
So, even though Justine thought it would be funny to advertise for a brown-eyed, blond-haired stud (which is an accurate
description of her prize-winning show dog), that was sure to
invite replies from men who wanted to tell us much, much
more about themselves than we would ever want to know. Ick.

✓ **Be descriptive and different.** For heaven's sake, everyone
loves walks on the beach at sunset. That doesn't tell the
reader anything about *you*. Ella showed her individuality
when she said she didn't harass animals or eat them. Karen's
description of herself as a world traveler, reader and gardener
told a lot about who she is. The ages, lifestyles and personalities of the women who were coerced into participating were
clear in the ads, which allowed people who might be a good
match to connect.

Did you ever see the movie *Grand Canyon*? It focuses on
two African American characters who are set up on a blind
date by their mutual friends. Quickly, the two characters realize they have nothing at all in common—they were just the
only two black people their friends knew.

If you're not careful, you can have the same dilemma when
you meet through a doggie personal ad. Denise did. Denise is

now happily married, but remembers placing a personal ad several years ago. She got a huge response, and some of the men were very nice—but none of them had a thing in common with her. There was no love connection. She later realized her mistake: Although she'd done a great job talking about dogs, she didn't give any details about herself. The only thing these men knew about Denise is that she liked dogs—and so they responded. She might have received fewer responses—but more intriguing ones—if she'd given a clue about her educational level, politics and lifestyle.

✓ **Be clever.** Consider some of these opening lines for your next personal ad:

"Lab seeks scientist . . ."

"Husky male seeks full-figured woman . . ."

"Golden retriever seeks lost soul . . ."

"Papillon seeks entomologist . . ."

"Afghan seeks couch potato . . ."

"Greyhound seeks bus driver . . ."

✓ **Have fun.** Go out with your friends and rate and rank the responses to your ad. Giggle. Enjoy.

✓ **Believe your dog.** This is where dog owners have an advantage over the rest of the world. Take the case of Rene. A few years ago, Rene ran what should have been the perfect ad to find a dog lover. The headline read: "Will you love me as much as my dog?" Then she listed some of Dakota's strong points: He was happy when he ate out of a can, he thought she was beautiful in the morning, he liked every color her hair had ever been. Rene found one of the respondents charming. Soon they were very involved, then they got engaged.

The problem: Believe it or not, the guy didn't like dogs, and especially didn't like Dakota—and Dakota didn't like him. Dakota gave the guy baleful stares and even growled under his breath. Rene eventually had to decide between her boyfriend and her dog.

She thought about which was nicer to her, and opted for the dog. Dakota was willing to make clear what Rene's friends were too polite to mention: Her boyfriend was an egocentric jerk. Eventually, Rene figured this out for herself.

The story has a happy ending. Rene is engaged again, to a dog-loving guy. This guy loves Dakota, and Dakota loves him. Not ever a stare or a snarl—just a warm, wagging tail. Rene and her fiancé have just bought a house with a huge fenced yard for Dakota, and are looking for a friendly Labrador Retriever to keep him company.

Chapter 17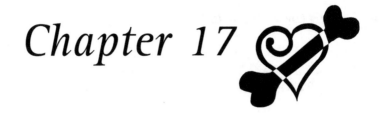

What Our Dogs Teach Us About Successful Relationships

You've probably seen this slogan written on T-shirts or bumper stickers: "The more I see of humans, the more I like my dog." This little aphorism seems to be proof that dog people aren't so good with humans.

Nothing could be further from the truth. Far more frequently, you'll find that nice people are well, nice people. They're kind and empathetic to animals, and they're considerate and loving to other humans.

If you doubt it for a second, consider what is undoubtedly the fastest-growing dog activity in America: animal-assisted therapy, where people and their pets visit hospitals, nursing homes, camps for

---

When Being a Nice Guy Can Lead to Romance

You don't have to have a hero dog to impress a potential love interest. Sometimes, you just have to be a nice guy.

"I never used a pet as date bait—but my Border Collie did lead me to romance," admits Marlowe. "Flash had somehow escaped from the yard, so we put an ad in the paper right away, along with all the other things you do looking for a dog. I met David when he responded to my ad—he had Flash! We started dating. It lasted seven years, and we are still friends."

You never know where your good deed will lead, do you?

---

disabled kids, and countless other locations where a warm smile and a cold nose make people happier. If you meet a genuine dog lover, it's likely you've met someone with a generous and gentle spirit.

Relating to People Using the Secrets of the Dog Trainers

There is a little glitch, however. It's a lot easier to relax around dogs than it is around people, even if you're an extrovert.

That's because dogs are nicer than people.

Dogs never make snotty comments about what you're wearing. They never, ever refuse to be seen with you in public because you don't have the best job in the world, or you gained 30 pounds, or you're in the middle of chemotherapy. They never throw some stupid thing you once said back in your face.

It's no wonder we feel more relaxed and confident when we're with our dogs.

Think just for a moment about your dog. Picture his sweet, lovable mug in front of you. Memorize how your face feels at that moment. Your eyes are wide open with a look of trust. You probably have a smile on your face. We know for a fact that your blood pressure is lower.

Now imagine meeting a blind date. Your eyes are probably either open wide in a state of semi-panic or slit closed with a look of skepticism. Are you smiling, or are your teeth a little bit clenched? And your heart is probably pounding so hard that you can hear it.

What would happen if you treated that blind date with as much openness and kindness as you treat a dog?

I have a (happily married) friend who has a job that requires him to be interviewed frequently by the media. He once confided to me that he just pretends the television reporter is his Newfoundland. He always looks happy, unshaken and really approachable on TV.

I first started using this concept in a job I had that required giving lots of presentations to local and state government boards and commissions—usually asking for funding for a nonprofit agency I managed. I can remember giving a presentation to the local County Commission, and envisioning which kind of dog each commissioner would be. One looked like a perky but scruffy terrier mix. Another had the stalwart look of a particularly dignified black Labrador. And one seemed to me to look like a poorly bred Collie, complete with a too-long nose and too-small, squinty eyes.

When I thought of them as dogs, I was so much less tense. My presentation was relaxed, smooth and compelling. And we got the funding we were seeking. (After making this admission, I just hope I can continue to make my living as a dog writer and never have to go back to that group of people to make a speech!)

Why not try envisioning your date as a dog? Don't think of the person you're seeing as a guy you're trying to impress or a woman you think you might not trust. Just envision a merry terrier or a friendly Beagle or a trustworthy Golden Retriever.

This advice is no stranger than all those people who tell you to envision an audience of naked people when you give a speech. (I always think how uncomfortable the seating looks for those poor naked rear ends. . . .)

If this advice can make you laugh at yourself, you're ahead of the game. And even if the date's a dud, at least you'll be amused.

Meeting People Using All Five Senses

You've probably heard stories—or even experienced—a dog who instinctively knew when someone was dangerous. We had the experience when I was a kid. Our Weimaraner, Cody, was a friendly, gentle family dog. He greeted everyone who came to the door with a wag and a welcome.

Except one day.

A man came to the door, telling my mother that he was selling vacuum cleaners. Cody came rushing to the door, the hair on his hackles raised. He bared his considerable teeth and snarled. He was ready to go after this total stranger.

My mother said, "No thanks" and slammed the door. She walked right to the phone and called the police, who sent a patrol car. As soon as they saw the man, they arrested him. He was wanted for a string of armed robberies.

Cody used all his senses when he met people, and he instantly knew this man wasn't a good guy. We can learn to do the same.

But first, a confession.

Cody wasn't the only dog in the Wood house when I was a kid. When I was eight years old, I spent the year as a Cocker Spaniel. It was easy for my parents to keep me entertained—they just had to throw a stick. I barked with enthusiasm when we went someplace in the car. When we went on a family swim outing, I'd only dog paddle, no matter how hard my father tried to show me the advantages of all the other strokes. (As if a Cocker Spaniel would do a backstroke—what was the man thinking?!)

I also learned to greet people like a dog. No, no, no. My mother didn't allow me to sniff anyone. But each person I'd meet, I'd open my large, brown Cocker Spaniel eyes, and look for the person behind

Lexiann and Jim: A True Love Story

Keisha, an Afghan Hound, had some issues with Lexiann's boyfriends. "After my divorce, Keisha, had absolutely no respect for any of the men I dated. She treated most of them as if they were the dirt beneath her feet."

Lexiann admits that aloofness is pretty typical Afghan behavior—but Keisha was intent on making her feelings known. "When she disliked one especially intensely, she would place herself between the guy and me. With men who were obsessed about their appearance, she wouldn't ignore them until she'd gotten fur on their clothing . . . then they became dirt beneath her feet."

This wasn't too upsetting to Lexiann, since she had absolutely no intention of getting involved in a serious relationship again. "Keisha's behavior helped with this," she says wryly.

"I was dating for fun only. I agreed to go out with Jim with zero intent of any type of involvement."

But something was decidedly different with this guy: Keisha went nuts. "She wagged her tail, leaned against him and, when he sat down, she laid her head in his lap," says Lexiann. "My father, who was there at the time and knew my feelings about not having a serious relationship, laughed and asked me what I was going to do about this one, since my dog seemed to like him.

Lexiann admits that Keisha was definitely an excellent judge of men. "Her attitude toward all my other dates had also been right on the mark about their personalities and their not being a good match for me. Jim turned out to be one of the good guys," she says.

Jim had grown up around dogs, because his parents' dogs were farm dogs, not house pets. But Keisha and Jim became close buddies, and Lexiann and Jim became soulmates. Jim went on to become involved in dog activities, including conformation showing, obedience and agility training and therapy visits.

"In a few months we will celebrate our 15th anniversary, and honestly, most of our time together has been filled with love and contentment," says Lexiann.

the face. And I'd perk up my large Cocker Spaniel ears (OK—my long, blonde pigtails) to hear their breathing and their heartbeat.

If we look at people though the eyes of a dog, we'll see them differently. We'll see beyond the good looks—or the not-so-good looks—and see their hearts. We'll hear more than their words—we'll understand their unspoken language, which screams out about whether they're kind or cruel.

If we let ourselves relax, we'll come closer to having the wisdom of our dogs when it comes to figuring out people.

Finding Your Inner Dog

Most people would not consider a Bouvier des Flandres to be the model of femininity. Bouviers are big, strong, tough dogs, bred to drive cattle to market and haul heavy loads in carts. They have wiry, tousled hair. To anyone but a Bouvier fancier, these dogs look something like an unmade bed.

But psychologist Joel Gavriele-Gold says his Bouvier Charlotte is a feminine archetype. "Charlotte's an Earth Mother," he says. She makes sure the two male dogs in her household come and go when they should. "She's on duty all the time, making sure everything's OK."

Maybe, says Gavriele-Gold, we can learn something from the way dogs play and love. That made me think about the lessons we can learn about gender and being comfortable in our own skin from our dogs.

 Dogs aren't confused by gender roles. Anyone who has watched their dogs closely can't help but notice the fact that the sexes each have their own behaviors. "I think dogs' gender roles teach us something. I do think there are sex differences that we should acknowledge and keep. There are some things that are basic to being male and female that we shouldn't try to neutralize and wash out," says Gavriele-Gold.

He says there are a handful of female roles and a handful of male roles in the dog world. For example, while his dog is an Earth Mother, my dog Goldie is most definitely of the Princess variety. I have to admit that I've watched Goldie with weird fascination for the decade that I've shared my life with her. Goldie is the girliest of girly-girls. Sometimes I think I should figure out a way to translate *The Feminine Mystique* into dog and give it to her to read.

Not only is Goldie the ultimate Princess, my male dogs Radar and Pogo are quintessential guys. Sometimes I expect to walk in the door and see them drinking beer and watching a football game on a large screen TV.

You think I'm exaggerating? Let me replay a scene that happens regularly at my house.

Goldie's favorite toy is lying on the floor. (OK, it's probably coincidence that it happens to be a little *pink* mouse.)

"Get your toy, Goldie," I say, thinking we'll have a rousing game of fetch just as soon as she brings it to me.

Goldie tilts her head as if to say, "I can't remember how to get my toy."

"Get your toy, Goldie," I say enthusiastically.

Head tilt.

"Come on Goldie, get your toy and then we'll play!"

Head tilt.

Finally, Radar can't stand it anymore. He's been quietly gnawing on a chew toy across the room. He sighs, gets up, brings me Goldie's toy, and then goes back to his own toy.

Obviously, it took a guy to solve the problem.

Dogs may have clear gender roles—but, unlike the roles sometimes imposed by human society, these gender roles are fair. The other Border Collies don't tell the girl dogs they can't herd sheep because of their gender, and nobody tells a male dog to hold in his emotions.

It's something to think about, isn't it?

Dogs are able to give and receive love. One of the reasons we get along so well with our dogs is that canines are great at relationships. Think about it: Dogs don't withhold love when they're angry. They don't sit and wait for you to figure out what's wrong. They ask for what they need from you—and they give you what you need from them.

And some people still call them the lesser species!

 Dogs greet the people they love with enthusiasm. When we come home, our dogs are waiting at the door, clearly and openly thrilled to see us. With a wagging tail and the nudge of a cold nose, they tell us just how important we are to them.

Think of doing the same thing for the people (and animals) you love. You don't have to fawn all over them—just smile, hug them, and say, "It's so nice to see you."

Do that for the people you care about, and I guarantee your life will be transformed.

 Dogs are playful, even flirtatious. "I love watching my dog Broodje when he wants to play with my female, Charlotte," says Gavriele-Gold. "He has the gracefulness of a horse in flight. Charlotte hides behind the trees, and then runs out at him. It's the kind of thing we've so outlawed in male-female relationships other than serious dating."

Watch your own dog in play, including the friendships he or she has with other dogs. Humans have nothing as elegant as a play bow—but think of the fun and joy you can have by just borrowing a little bit of that honest sense of fun of a dog at play.

 Express yourself. Think about how you're able to express yourself in your relationship with your dog, and consider applying some of those lessons to the humans in your life.

For example, Lucinda was a successful, aloof, driven woman. She had the perfect, stark, modern home—all polished chrome and angles. Then a little terrier came into her life. She started to play with this little guy, throwing his toys and joyfully playing tug of war.

Soon, her neighbors noticed a startling difference in Lucinda. She laughed and said hello. She was warmer and friendlier. She'd learned a lot about behavior from her dog. If you asked Lucinda, she probably wouldn't have even realized she'd changed. But her friends and neighbors sure saw the difference.

I've known people who were phobic about driving, and even leaving their homes, who caught the dog show "bug"— and found themselves traveling around the world to shows.

Another friend has American Staffordshire Terriers, one of the so-called Pit Bull breeds. She was determined that her dogs would be the kind of goodwill ambassadors that would show people that this breed can be a wonderful pet and companion. She started doing agility with her dogs—and lost 100 pounds. Today's she's an athletic, strong person—the perfect reflection of her dogs.

Another friend was painfully shy until she started doing animal-assisted therapy with her Golden Retriever, Sunny. "Sunny showed me what to do," says Margie. This woman is now in training for crisis response—next time there's a disaster, she and her dog will be on hand to comfort victims.

I even know a man who credits his dog for helping him learn to pick better women for relationships. "I'd always picked killer women and nurturing dogs," he says. "After about 200 years of psychotherapy, that's finally changed. I wonder if having my perfectly adoring female dogs who knew how to give love to me and take love from me has taught me how a give and take of love should feel."

There is an old dog trainer's creed: Let me be the kind of person that my dog thinks I am. Taking a step beyond that, maybe we can become with humans the same kind of person we are with our dogs: gentler, funnier, sunnier, more trusting and more trustworthy.

And, next time I go shopping, I'm going to buy the kind of outfit that Goldie would suggest I wear. I have a feeling it's pink—and might be decorated with rhinestones.

Chapter 18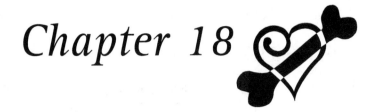

Road Trip!

The road trip! There's nothing more quintessentially American. But sometimes singles cheat themselves out of this adventure because they don't have anyone to share the fun with. If you have a dog, you aren't alone. Dogs can be the world's best traveling companions.

Forget Jack Kerouac's *On the Road*. Our style is more like *Travels With Charley*, the story of John Steinbeck and his Poodle. (Take the book along to read on your trip; it's the only cheerful thing Steinbeck ever wrote.)

You and your dog can have huge amounts of fun exploring new places and meeting new people. Who knows what cowgirl or cowboy you might meet in Texas, or urban sophisticate you and your dog will find in New York?

So load the car with suitcases, blankets, food, toys—oh, and a couple of things for the human—and get ready for adventure.

Plan Ahead

If you're traveling by yourself, you might not bother to make motel reservations. If you're traveling with your dog, don't take the chance of being stranded without a dog-friendly room.

Happily, it's easy to make reservations in motels that cater to canines. There are several sites on the Internet that provide information about dog-friendly travel. The most comprehensive is Petswelcome.com. It provides detailed information on more than 25,000 pet-friendly hotels, bed and breakfasts, ski resorts, campgrounds and beaches. And that's not all. It also has a special section for places that are big-dog friendly. And it has a section called Fun & Cool Places in which dog-loving travelers report on especially great local attractions, including dog-friendly dining, dog parks and stores that welcome dogs. You can get most of this information in the book version of *The Portable Petswelcome.com* (Howell Book House).

Local communities now provide a lot of information on the Internet, as well. Type in the name of your destination in an Internet search engine, and odds are you can find a host of information about the place, including local parks and their regulations (or at least a contact who can tell you if dogs are welcome).

So you and your dog should get out the map and dream big!

Safety on the Road

While traveling with your dog is a great way to meet new people all across the country, use common sense.

- ✗ **Don't leave your dog in an unlocked car—even for a moment.** An acquaintance of mine went into a service station to pay for her gas. When she returned, her little dog was gone. He'd been stolen by thieves in the mere moments she was in the store. Don't let the same thing happen to you.

- ✓ **Make sure your dog is wearing ID.** Preferably, both tags and a microchip (which can't come off).

✓ **Bring complete medical records with you, including the dog's vaccine record (especially for rabies).** If you are taking a long trip across state lines, you should have your veterinarian complete a health certificate for your dog.

✓ **Use a crate.** People wear seatbelts—dogs need to travel in a safe crate. Airbags can kill small dogs, just as they can kill babies. Keep your dog in the backseat for safety.

Motel Petiquette

Motels aren't required to accept dogs. They do it because it's worth it to them financially, or because the person who makes the decisions is a dog lover. Don't betray their trust.

✗ **Don't leave your dog alone in the room.** It's not fair to the other guests if your dog decides to bark in a new place.

✓ **Be fastidiously clean.** Start your trip with a clean dog, and bathe him at a local dog wash if he gets dirty along the way (*not* in the motel bathtub!). If he's on the bed, cover it with a sheet from home so he doesn't shed hair and dander on the bed. (Remember, the next guest might be violently allergic to dogs.)

✓ **If you think your dog might mark territory, plan ahead.** You can buy "cummerbunds" for male dogs who mark; these are basically absorbent undergarments for dogs. (One source is www.fidogear.com.) The staff and subsequent guests shouldn't have to deal with lingering odors and stains.

✓ **Only use designated potty areas.** And don't forget to scoop.

With a modicum of planning, you and your dog can have a blast on the open road. You can use all your fun tricks to meet people. And your dog will have new audiences to dazzle in every city.

Life can indeed be good.

Chapter 19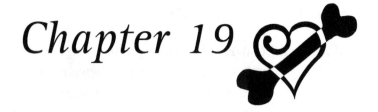

The First Date

So, all the advice has worked. You've been out there circulating with your dog. You met a nice man or woman and you're ready for the first date. Why not make it a dog-friendly experience?

Go for a Walk

"I ran a personal ad that said I liked dogs—and I got about 20 responses," says Miranda, who had two Labrador Retrievers at the time. "I picked seven guys to meet. I made dates with each one to walk my dogs. I figured it killed two birds with one stone: My dogs got their exercise, and I could see how well he did with my dogs."

The walk doesn't have to be in your neighborhood. Think of a trendy downtown neighborhood, or a dog-friendly hiking trail, or a quaint little town that has a pretty river walk. Plan to take the dogs wherever you'd like to explore—but check ahead to make sure your well-behaved pets are welcome. Oh—and if the romance gets serious—just be aware that Tiffany and Company in New York welcomes dogs in the world's most famous jewelry store.

If you both have dogs, this first date does something more: It helps cement your dogs' friendship. The best way for dogs to learn to like each other (as long as they are controllable on leash) is for them to go on a walk together. The mere act of walking together creates the feeling of a pack.

Not only is this a great start for your dogs, it's a good way for couples to get acquainted with less stress. Your dogs have therapeutic value: Your heart rate will be lower, your stress hormones more normal. You'll be more relaxed and better able to just enjoy the day.

This is the ideal first date for dog-lovers—and might be a step toward becoming just plain lovers.

Schedule a Play Date

Maybe you met someone at the dog park or puppy kindergarten class, and want to go to the next level. Schedule a play date for your compatible canines. Be sure to plan ahead, in case you don't want the date to end too soon—bring plenty of water and some snacks for the dogs. You might want to throw a comfy blanket in the car so your dog has a place to curl up with his pal, while you and the object of your affections take some time to become better acquainted.

Go to a Dog Show

You'll have to leave your own dogs at home for this one, but it can be fun. You won't run out of things to talk about as the amazing array of dogs goes prancing by you.

Don't forget the best-kept secret of dog shows: They have the coolest stuff to buy in the world. Everything from several T-shirts for each breed to incredible leashes and collars to fabulous dog books to antique collectibles to 14-karat gold fine jewelry in every breed to bumper stickers that say things like "It's Hard to Be Humble When

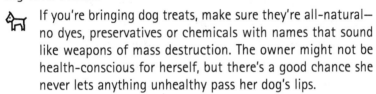

Forget Chocolates—Think Dog Treats

Are you the romantic sort who likes to show up with a sweet bouquet of flowers? If you really want to impress a dog-lover, show up with something for the dog. Here are some hints that will help melt a dog-lover's heart.

- If you're bringing dog treats, make sure they're all-natural—no dyes, preservatives or chemicals with names that sound like weapons of mass destruction. The owner might not be health-conscious for herself, but there's a good chance she never lets anything unhealthy pass her dog's lips.

- Make sure any plush toys are dog-safe—no plastic eyes that a puppy can pull off and swallow; no tiny parts.

- Think about whether the present is appropriate for the size, age and breed of dog. A Chihuahua isn't likely to play with a tennis ball, and a Great Dane might swallow a small toy. They say it's the thought that counts, and the more thought you put into trying to make this a present the dog will like, the more it will count.

You Own a Petit Basset Griffon Vendeen" to the most incredible array of dog toys under one roof, dog shows are a shopper's paradise.

One word of warning: Not everyone views dog shows in the same way. If you find a Poodle in show coat gorgeous and your date starts laughing hysterically, you might not be a match. If you think well-bred dogs are a valuable addition to canine history and your date thinks closed gene pools are a travesty against nature, you might not have a good time at a dog show.

Go to a Dog-Friendly Diner or Coffeehouse

The traditional first date is meeting for a casual dinner or going to a trendy spot for a pricey latte. If you have well-behaved dogs, you can bring them with you—as long as you and the dogs are outside, and the restaurant or coffee bar doesn't mind.

What better way is there to spend a summer afternoon than sipping a beverage of your choice, flirting with someone you find attractive, while your dog soaks up the sunshine with you?

This plan can go horribly awry, however. Think before you invite your dogs out to dinner. Are the dogs compatible—or will they be snarling at each other under the table? Do you have placid old dogs who'd enjoy a long afternoon just hanging out—or young dogs who would be squirming and barking, looking for action? Only bring the pooches with you if they have the training and temperament to think this is a good time.

Puppies and Panties

Anyone who has ever had a dog knows that puppies are fixated on underwear, especially ladies' panties. The theory goes that the more something smells like the pup's owner, the more the puppy wants to play with it. And nothing smells more like you than yesterday's unmentionables.

Maria was thrilled when Brad asked her out. He was smart, very attractive and a nice guy. "He was kind of a reach for me—better looking than other guys I'd dated," admits Maria. But the date was going well. They'd gone out to dinner, and she asked him back to her place for a cup of coffee and some flirting.

In an instant, the romantic moment was gone. In rushed Maria's Great Dane puppy, with a pair of panties on her head. "They weren't my pretty, low-cut, silk panties—they were my big, oversized cotton underwear, the kind with ugly flowers," Maria remembers.
The date was over. Brad never called again.

Maria is philosophical. "The dog did look funny. If he couldn't laugh at that, he wasn't worth it." Then she pauses. "But he sure was cute."

Go to a Charity Event

There are countless fundraisers for good animal causes. There are walk-a-thons (usually your dog is welcome), auctions and dances (inevitably called the Fur-ball). Especially if you work or volunteer for the charity, this is a perfect opportunity invite someone along. It's less scary than a "real" date—after all, it's important for everyone to attend, and the money goes to charity. If you're a woman asking a man out, inviting him to an event for organization is both flattering and nonthreatening to him, plus you have the security of knowing this is your "territory" (dogs are not the only ones who feel most relaxed on their own turf), and you're surrounded by your friends.

Go for it!

Chapter 20

Using Your Dog to End a Bad Date

Not every date works out well. Sometimes we just don't click with someone. Sometimes, as we get to know a person, life in solitary confinement seems a better alternative than a second date. Everyone needs an exit strategy to end the date from hell. Your dog can be the key to that strategy.

If you think this idea is a modern one, just read a little mythology. Artemis, the ancient Greek goddess of the hunt, used a pack of dogs to end a date—permanently. The story goes that Artemis and some of her favorite nymphs were bathing nude. A young hunter named Actaeon (who was old enough to know better) came upon the goddess and her retinue. Artemis, a major figure in the pantheon of Greek gods, was worried about ruining her reputation—she was afraid that Actaeon (who apparently was something of a cad) would boast of seeing her naked body.

So Artemis did what major goddesses do—she turned the puny mortal into a stag. Not surprisingly, Actaeon fled in fear—and he could move pretty darn fast now he was a deer. Unfortunately for poor Actaeon, his own pack of dogs spotted him running. Hunting dogs will be hunting dogs, so after a long chase the dogs caught Actaeon, tore him to shreds and devoured his flesh.

Yikes!

You can end a date effectively without exhibiting the wrath of a vengeful goddess. Here are some nonviolent ways to use your dog to cut short a not-so-romantic interlude.

 The Corgi who held her breath. Joan and her Corgi, Sneakers, were totally in tune with one another. This was especially helpful when it was time to send a date home who was overstaying his welcome.

"Sneakers could tell when I thought it was time for the guy to go home," says Joan. Sneakers would come up to the couch and stare at Joan. Now, Sneakers had developed a habit over the years of holding her breath when she wanted to go outside. So there was Sneakers, staring at Joan and the date, holding her little Corgi breath. After a bit, she'd exhale loudly then hold her breath again.

"It's hard to ignore a dog holding her breath," says Joan with a laugh. "I'd say, 'Poor Sneakers really, really has to go outside.'" So Joan was up, letting the dog out, turning on the bright lights and giving her date his coat.

Much more subtle than Artemis, yet still effective.

 The dog with gas. Oh, don't tell me you haven't already thought of this one!

Jason admits to using this technique. "My Cattle Dog, Mattie, really likes vegetables, but some of them give her horrific gas,"he says. Feed your dog some cabbage or green peppers and the date will decide it's time to go home on her own.

Think of it as biological warfare.

Of course, doggie gas isn't exactly a "smart bomb." And, in some dogs, it's just a fact of life, 365 days a year. Anyone who loves a Bulldog knows that an acute sense of smell and a Bulldog aren't a good combination. And maybe that tolerant woman who doesn't mind the gas is the perfect person for you and your flatulent four-legged friend.

Bark on command. This is easy to teach, and can always come in handy. No one will make google eyes at you for long with a dog staring and yapping at the two of you. What your date won't know is that *you* told your dog to bark.

Here's the easiest way to teach a dog to speak on command: Catch your dog in the act of barking and reward him. So when the dog starts to bark, say "good speak!" and give him a doggie cookie. After you've done that several times, say "speak!" If he responds with a bark, reward him lavishly. If he hasn't figured out what you want, keep rewarding him when he barks until he understands that "speak!" and the act of barking are paired—and are accompanied by a reward. (See the Appendix for more information.)

Of course, you can't be sitting at the dinner table with your date, turn to your dog and say "speak!" Well, you can—but it's not the kind of smooth and subtle move I expect from you.

Here's what you do: Instead of teaching the dog to bark at the traditional word "speak," choose another word—one that you can work into a conversation but don't use regularly in everyday speech. Like, maybe "sauerbraten." So you can casually say, "I'm glad you liked the hamburgers I bought at 7-11. My real specialty is cooking *sauerbraten*, though." At that point, your dog will start barking!

You can use any word you want. So if you really do cook sauerbraten, maybe your word for "speak" is "petunias." (As in, "I can't believe it's already December. Just think, it'll be time to plant my *petunias* in only three months!)

The possibilities are endless. Just pick any word that might fit smoothly into a conversation and train that as your "speak" word. (A list of possible "speak" commands include "Pythagorean theorem," "duct tape," "macarena," "Twiggy," "quagmire," "cockroach," "truculent," "liposuction," "stalactite"—the sort of words you can always slip into polite conversation.)

Lifting a leg on your date. Don't worry—this is just a little doggie acting, not the real thing!

No one wants to be peed on by a dog. It "marks" you as, well, pretty darn low on the status levels of both humans and dogs. So a date who even imagines that he or she might receive this major insult will instantly head for home.

To teach a dog to look like he's lifting his leg, just tickle the bottom of his back foot. As he begins to raise his paw, say, "Good whoops!" and reward him. Soon he should be lifting his back leg reliably when you say "whoops!"

Note: For the sake of your carpet, never, ever use this command when your dog is actually peeing or about to pee. The idea is that the leg lift looks like the dog is about to pee, but the dog never associates the movement of his leg with actually going potty. Otherwise, this little joke is on you!

Once you have a dog who's trained to lift his leg when you say "whoops!" you have your exit strategy. When your guest is hanging around too long, call your dog over and pet him next to your date. When the dog is near the date's leg, get a startled look on your face and say "Whoops! I think Spot is about to pee on you!" The date will look down at a dog whose back leg is balanced delicately in the air.

Your evening from hell will be over.

Show teeth. This is some more doggie acting that even the friendliest dog can happily learn. Doggie teeth are scary—

*Baebe belongs to Paula Ratoza, who has
taught her to show her teeth on command.
It's a quick way to get rid of a bad date.*

even if you own a small dog. If you own a big, strapping
Rottweiler, Doberman Pinscher or Pit Bull, the sight of those
teeth will strike fear into the heart of even the bravest date.

Paula Ratoza, who owns the Feathers & Fur Talent Agency,
has taught many animal actors to show their teeth. She says
the best way to do it is to playfully push your hand at the
dog's nose, saying "got your nose!"

"The dog will pull back his lips to get his nose away from
your fingers," explains Ratoza. Soon, he'll pull back his lips
on cue—and you have a dog who looks like he's about to
attack (except for the happy, wagging tail—since he thinks
he's playing a game).

Of course, never, ever play this game with a dog who has aggression issues or one who doesn't like things in his face. This is supposed to be a game of *pretend* aggression!

Dogs can do it all. They can attract a mate and help get rid of a nuisance. Is there no end to their magic?

Chapter 21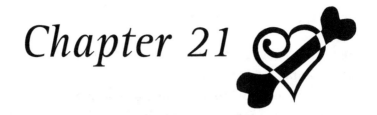

Compatible Pets and Partners (Including the Compatibility Quiz)

The problem with meeting someone attractive is that we mere humans too often throw all our common sense out the window.

Turn on the AM radio, flick on daytime TV talk shows or read the Living section of your newspaper, and you'll be deluged by psychologists and relationship experts pleading for people to slow down and think. Is this potential lover really compatible? Do you share the same values? Can you get along with each other after the hormones subside?

Dog lovers have all these concerns—and more. In addition to everything else, you have to ask yourself if the person a good match for your pet. At least as important is the question, are your new love's pets compatible with yours? Life isn't any fun if you're truly afraid your partner's dog will hurt yours.

Here are some points to ponder as you make eyes at the newcomer to the dog park who's walking that cute Golden Retriever:

1. **Do dogs play the same role in our lives?** For some of us, dogs are family. They aren't merely a diversion until we get "real kids" and they aren't a substitute for friends. They are so much a part of us that we can't quite breathe if they're at the veterinarian or boarding at a kennel.

   If you feel this way about your dog, you are going to have a conflict with someone who says her pet is "just a dog." Don't ignore the queasy feeling in your gut if you don't think you two share the same vision of a dog's value in your home. And for heaven's sake, don't wait to talk about it until after the wedding—when he thinks the dog should sleep outside and you think the dog belongs in your bed.

2. **Do we have compatible discipline/training styles?** Dog discipline (like child discipline) can cause huge arguments. If one of you thinks that it's adorable when Fluffy jumps on you and the other thinks he should be belted for the same behavior, you have a problem. Sometimes, the difference in styles comes from experiencing different kinds of training (he went to a cookies-and-clicker trainer; she went to a jerk-and-pull trainer 15 years ago). Talk about your differences and see if you can compromise—or even convince the other that your (preferably gentle, humane) training style is best.

3. **Are the dogs compatible?** There are a lot of high prey drive breeds that generally aren't recommended to live with little dogs. To a Siberian Husky, for example, a jumping, running little Papillon pretty much looks like a rabbit. And most Huskies want to kill rabbits.

   Sometimes the problem can be solved by training and maturing. It's likely that a rambunctious, rowdy Golden

Retriever puppy will eventually be a calm and steady companion to a little dog—but not necessarily.

One advantage of meeting over dogs—rather than over children—is that you can size up these canine compatibility problems early in the relationship. When people have two-legged kids, you might not meet her child for six months—only to find out the kid likes to light fires. . . .

4. **Look for signs of cruelty.** The way a dog interacts with his owner can give you a lot of information. Recently, I was doing an obedience demonstration with my dog Pogo. I was waving my hand around his face—and it suddenly dawned on me that Pogo wasn't flinching, wasn't even blinking. He had complete faith in me, and absolutely no experience with violence. It never occurred to Pogo that my flailing hand was any kind of threat.

   Dogs—like people—are all "wired" differently. A dog who has been given the finest, most loving care might still flinch from a moving hand near his face. Nonetheless, trust and faith are transparent in dogs. I want a man in my life whose dog trusts him as much as Pogo trusts me.

5. **Red flags.** Do you completely trust the other person with your dog, or are you a little worried? Do you harbor fears that your new beau might hurt your dog? Do you worry he or she might be so irresponsible that the dog will get loose through a door or gate? Think about it. If you have these doubts, what kind of long-term partner will this person be? Break off the relationship before it gets even more complicated.

The Good News

While you need to keep an eye out for danger signs in a relationship, the good news is that your dog-lover lover has a good chance of being a great mate. People with pets, on average, make more money than those who don't have pets, are more stable in their employment, and are healthier.

- A pet-lover's kindness to animals usually translates into compassion for people.
- The patience to train and care for an animal often shows itself in patience with people.
- It takes empathy to understand what a dog needs and make sure those needs are met. This empathetic person might apply those skills to you—even when you're not sure what's bothering you.
- Gentleness to animals can also manifest itself in a gentle, nurturing relationship with another person.

Step-Dogs

Sweet success!

You've met the person of your dreams. You're seriously involved, and life is going to end happily ever after. You think a lot about what your partner needs and wants, but are you thinking about their dog?

- You owe your partner's dog respect. The dog deserves the chance to maintain her relationship with your partner without sabotage. Believe it or not, it's common for people to feel jealous of the time their partner gives a pet. Instead of feeling jealousy, spend that time staying bonded with your own pet.
- Don't be in too big a hurry to have "our" dogs. If both of you come into the relationship with your own pets, it's not always wise to lump them together, especially early in the relationship. If you merge your canine pack early and then the relationship doesn't last, you have incredibly complicated emotional ties to break with your ex-partner's dogs. I actually know people who have custody of their Labrador Retriever every other week. If

you have one partner with a clear attachment to a particular dog and the other with primary attachments to a different dog, these messy situations can be minimized.

Discuss your pets' behavior, from squabbling among the dogs to agreeing on whether or not dogs sleep in the bed. You need to agree how to handle these issues. Call in a trainer or animal behaviorist if you need help.

The Compatibility Quiz

1. Dating puts demands on our time. Since the relationship started:
   a. We both manage to spend the majority of our nonworking time with our dogs, either together or separately.
   b. One of us spends a lot more time with our dogs than the other—and that's causing some friction.
   c. I have to admit that since we've found human companionship, we both spend lot less time with our dogs.

2. When it comes to training and disciplining the dogs:
   a. Our discipline is very different—one of us is much more harsh; the other much more permissive.
   b. One of us is a lot better at consistently training dogs and has pretty much taken over the role of trainer for all the dogs.
   c. Our training styles are pretty much the same.

3. When the dogs are together:
   a. It's worrisome—we fear they might hurt each other.
   b. They're the best buddies! We're not sure where the human relationship will end up, but the dogs will certainly be friends for life.
   c. They pretty much ignore each other.

4. When one of us is busy and the dogs need puppy-sitting:

   a. We don't ever puppy-sit each other's dogs—one of us would feel terrible if something happened to the other's dog.

   b. We watch each other's dogs—why not leave your dog with the person you trust most in the world?

   c. One of us can watch dogs, but not the other. We must admit, one of us is a bit of an "airhead"—and might leave the door or gate open. The other one doesn't make those kinds of mistakes.

5. When we interact with each other's dogs:

   a. One of us treats our own dogs much better than our partner's—and the other partner treats both sets of "fur kids" the same.

   b. We each treat our own dogs noticeably better than we treat our partner's.

   c. Dogs are dogs—we treat them all well!

6. When it comes to how our dogs spend most of their time:

   a. They're both indoor dogs—with lots of walks and activities!

   b. Both dogs stay outside mostly—of course, we make sure they have a warm place to stay and plenty of food and water.

   c. One person's dog is an indoor dog; the other person has an outside dog.

7. When it comes to veterinary care:

   a. Neither of us has thought a lot about veterinary costs. Can this get expensive?

   b. We both would figure out a way to pay for whatever the dog needed—after all, that's what you do for family.

   c. We have different philosophies: One of us says the sky's the limit; the other one says it's only practical to pay just so much and no more.

8. When we're smooching on the couch:
   a. The dogs are someplace else. They go nuts when we touch each other.
   b. The dogs are content; they seem to sense this is a good thing. If they get a little rowdy, we make sure they're OK and put them in a crate with a favorite toy.
   c. Who can concentrate? The dogs get into mischief every time we close our eyes to kiss!

Scoring

1. a. 3	b. 1	c. 2
2. a. 1	b. 2	c. 3
3. a. 1	b. 3	c. 2
4. a. 2	b. 3	c. 1
5. a. 1	b. 2	c. 3
6. a. 3	b. 2	c. 1
7. a. 2	b. 3	c. 1
8. a. 1	b. 3	c. 2

Interpreting Your Score

18-24: The humans and dogs in this relationship are living harmoniously. You mostly agree about how dogs should be treated in the household. The dogs generally behave well together, and most important of all, you trust the other human. This relationship has promise!

12-17: It's time to sit down and talk. You have some different views about the role of dogs in your life—and it's already causing friction. Still, there's enough common ground that you have the opportunity to learn from each other and develop shared values.

0-11: Uh-oh. One of you considers dogs to be family, and the other sees them as man's best acquaintance. Look long and hard at what life would be like together before getting serious.

Questions of Special Concern

Did you score a 1 on questions 3, 4 or 6? These are questions that might suggest a serious roadblock ahead in the relationship—even if your other scores were good.

Question 3. This question looks at the relationship between the dogs. If you answered (a), seek professional help right away. Meanwhile, keep these dogs separated. Wishing and hoping they'll get along won't solve the problem. And you will never forgive yourselves if one of your dogs seriously hurts the other.

Question 4. This question explored how well you trust each other with your dogs. If you answered (c), you have a serious imbalance in your relationship. Either one of you is unfairly criticizing the other ("S/He's such a goofball, he can't even watch my dog for an hour!"), or one of you is sabotaging the safety of the other's dog. In either case, you need to examine why one of you in the relationship is considered trustworthy, and the other isn't.

Question 6. This one asks if you have indoor or outdoor dogs. If you answered (c), you are probably headed for a showdown. Usually, people with outdoor dogs view them as pets or even property, and people with indoor dogs consider them family members. If your dog is important to you—she shares your bed, your secret hopes, your secret fears—you aren't likely to put her outside to live. You won't understand someone who treats their dog that way—and what are you going to do when you're in a committed relationship with each other and your new spouse announces that your dog belongs outside? Think about it.

When a Dog Problem Isn't a Problem Dog

Sometimes you might find yourself having horrendous arguments about a pet. These arguments aren't always really about the dog, explains Dr. Joel Gavriele-Gold, a clinical psychologist who has practiced in Manhattan for nearly 30 years. He says a dog can become a proxy for the couple's discontent.

Here are some warning signs that counseling might be necessary to solve a problem:

- ✗ **Violence toward an animal.** You can't solve this yourself. Any adult (or child) who hurts an animal needs to see a qualified therapist.

- ✗ **Jealousy and control.** "Shelter workers say an unbelievable number of pets are turned in because people are told they have to make a choice between a pet and a significant other," says Gavriele-Gold. No one who truly loves you would force you to make that choice.

- ✗ **Complaining rather than training.** Often, people know what will cure a pet's behavior problem, but don't implement the training plan. Rather than solve the problem, they may want the dog to continue to act her part in the family drama. "The idea of a pet's behavior change can be very threatening," says Dr. Mary Lee Nitschke, a psychologist and animal behaviorist.

The Bottom Line

You were attracted to each other because of your pets. You and your partner need to work cooperatively to make sure, at a minimum, your pets' lives are as good as they were before you became involved. If you need to bring in help—whether it's a trainer or a psychologist, do what you have to so your pets can feel safe and secure.

If your pets are happy, the odds are good your relationship will endure and flourish.

Chapter 22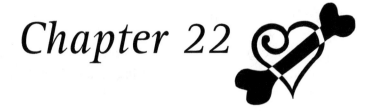

Dogs on the Bed

There's no topic more hotly debated than dogs on the bed. Especially as a couple is becoming newly intimate, the bed takes on a lot of emotional significance.

But sleeping with your dog can have emotional significance, too. After all, you might have shared a bed for a decade or more. It feels disloyal to kick the dog out now.

There is no one right or wrong answer about dogs in the bed. Here are some things to consider:

- If there are no behavior problems (such as growling or other signs of a power struggle) with the dog of *either partner*, and if *both* partners want one or more dogs on the bed, that's fine.

- If the dog isn't going to sleep on the bed, that's also fine. Let the dog stay in the room—dogs feel more secure when they're with their pack. Give each dog a comfortable crate, with snuggly bedding and with doors that close.

🐕 If you're going to be up late, uh . . . well, you know what I mean—give the dogs something to do. Give them a bone to chew or a toy to play with. It's not like they're going to go to sleep before you're . . . uh, quiet.

Quiz

Does Your Dog Belong on the Bed?

1. My dog growls at my partner or me when he doesn't get his way.

    Yes ___   No ___

2. I try not to move in bed, because my dog gets cranky if I do.

    Yes ___   No ___

3. My dog has peed in or on the bed in the last month.

    Yes ___   No ___

4. My dog often doesn't come when I call him—unless he knows for a fact I've got food in my hand.

    Yes ___   No ___

5. I feel lucky that I get part of the bed—the dog won't let anyone on his chair.

    Yes ___   No ___

If you answered "yes" to any of these questions, it's time to get the dog off the bed, at least temporarily.

In the wild, the alpha dog (the top dog in the pack) decides where the other dogs will sleep. He picks the best spot, and all the other dogs arrange themselves around him. In your house, the bed is that best spot. So when he takes the bed, your dog is declaring that he's in charge and you're not.

Whether or not your dog belongs on the bed at night depends on how he acts with you all day long. If you have a dog who otherwise listens to you and who happily moves on and off the bed when you ask him to, go ahead and sleep with your dog. I do!

But "yes" answers to any of the questions in the quiz indicate you've got a power struggle going on—and you're losing it. Here's what those "yes" answers meant:

Question 1: Any dog who is growling at people is in trouble. He's certainly trying to run things—and he isn't doing a very good job of it. Call a trainer or animal behaviorist this instant. I'm not kidding! Put the book down and get help. He certainly doesn't belong on the bed until the situation is under control.

Question 2: Your dog may be an angel all day, but if he gets cranky when you move in bed, he's off for at least three days. He can sleep in a comfy crate, and not have his sleep disturbed.

Question 3: Peeing on the bed, especially if it's new behavior, could be a sign that your dog is in a power struggle with your new partner. The dog is off the bed until the issues are resolved.

Also, take your dog to the veterinarian for a check-up. Inappropriate urination can have many physical causes including a bladder infection and canine cognitive dysfunction. However, keep the dog off the bed until you know what has triggered the peeing.

Question 4: When your dog doesn't come when called, he's telling you that he makes the decision about when he comes and goes—not you. You need some training help. And don't invite the dog onto the bed until the issue is resolved.

Question 5: A dog who declares his favorite chair off-limits is also calling the shots. It's time to call a professional trainer. No bed privileges until the behavior ends.

If you both have happy, generally well-behaved dogs, and you want to sleep with them, I say go ahead. You just might need a bigger bed.

Chapter 23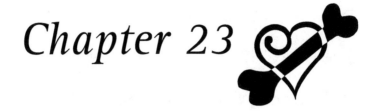

What Happens if Love Doesn't Nuzzle Its Way Into Your Heart

So, you've run the personal ads and schmoozed at the dog park. Your dog rolls over, plays dead and has hip political humor. You've traveled to every dog-friendly diner in North America.

And—you're still dateless.

Cheer up. It could be worse.

Love gone wrong has its advantages. You can wear one of those cheesy T-shirts that says, "The more I know about men [or women], the more I like my dog."

You can post lists to the Internet, like these:

10 Reasons Why a Dog Is Better Than a Man

1. Male dogs aim accurately when they pee.
2. Dogs like your cooking.
3. Dogs never think your favorite pair of sweat pants makes you look fat.
4. Dogs like your mother.
5. Dogs never think you'd look better with a boob job.
6. Dogs leave you half the bed.
7. Dogs know that "no" means "no."
8. Dogs like to help around the house on weekends.
9. Dogs never have a younger, cuter owner in the wings, just in case it doesn't work out with you.
10. It's legal to neuter them.

10 Reasons Why a Dog Is Better Than a Woman

1. Dogs love to watch football on TV. (It's not a coincidence that there are teams called the Huskies and the Bulldogs.)
2. Dogs never ask you if an outfit makes them look fat.
3. Dogs don't ever think you need to talk things out—again.
4. Dogs like the same jokes, over and over and over again. Good dog!
5. Except for a lap or two of toilet water, dogs leave the bathroom to you. You won't ever find dogs leaving pantyhose hanging in the shower.
6. Dogs never suggest that their mother moves in with you.

7. Dogs never borrow your razor without permission to shave their legs.

8. Dogs know you still love them, even if you say another dog is pretty.

9. Dogs never give you the silent treatment.

10. Three little letters: PMS.

It can be kind of fun to completely give yourself over to cynicism. OK—are we past that now?

The Truth

Even if you don't succeed in finding a two-legged love interest with this book, you haven't failed. After all, you're having great adventures with your dog.

If you read a diet book and don't lose weight, all you have at the end is your extra pounds, and yourself. If the advice doesn't pan out too well in a conventional dating book, all you have are a few weird stories, and yourself. If you go to yet another self-help seminar and it doesn't change your life, all you have is a vocabulary full of psychobabble, and yourself. And if you're spending your weekends in sports bars dreaming of a date, all you have is a hangover—and yourself.

But with this book, even if you don't find romance from a two-legged love, you did learn about loyalty, communication and companionship from the four-footed love of your life. If you take your dog on more walks, groom him more beautifully, teach him tricks, and maybe volunteer at an animal shelter or do animal-assisted therapy at a hospital, that makes your life better and more complete—and you have more than yourself.

Love is where we find it in this lifetime. Our dogs are our companions, friends and family. We're not so eager to move into a relationship with the wrong man or woman when we have a dog in the house, welcoming us home and making it clear that he thinks humans are minor deities. Life could be much worse.

So go out and have fun with your dog. You might find human love in all the dog places—or you might find that love is a four-footed creature who loves you with all his heart.

That's the joy of life with a dog. Even if you don't find a human to share your home, you're never alone.

Appendix

Training Fundamentals

Throughout this book, you'll see several ideas for teaching tricks to your dog. Instructions on how to teach the trick are given in the text, but there are some general principles to keep in mind.

- Tricks should be fun for you and your dog. This isn't a "do it or die" situation—it's the canine equivalent of a joke. So treat it that way. Laugh with your dog, enjoy the moment. This is part of the pleasure of hanging out with your dog.

- Use positive training methods. This isn't a time for choke collars, prong collars and jerking leashes. This is the time for cookies, praise and cheers.

- Don't ask your dog to do any trick that is dangerous, too strenuous for his particular build and abilities, or makes him feel worried or anxious. It's supposed to be fun for him, too!

- Most tricks are taught by catching your dog doing something right, and marking that moment with a clicker or special word.

163

Using a Clicker to Teach Tricks

Clickers are little noise-making devices you can hold in your hand; most trick trainers and Hollywood trainers use them. Clickers make a distinctive "click" sound (you might have guessed that!) when you press them. Clicker advocates say a clicker is almost like a separate language for dogs and other animals.

To clicker-train a behavior, follow these steps:

1. Teach your dog the magic of the clicker.

    Teach the dog that a click is connected with a reward. So you click and treat, click and treat, click and treat. Very quickly, your dog will hear the click and turn to you with a happy face and a wagging tail. He now has learned that the sound of the click is a magic and joyful noise!

    While you don't have to use a clicker, you do need something with a distinct sound. So you can click the top of a ballpoint pen or use the lid of a Snapple bottle (or any other bottle lid that pops up and down). It needs to be a clear, quick, noise that sounds different from anything else. That is why clicker trainers don't suggest that people use their voice.

2. Teach your dog a trick using a clicker.

    After your pooch has learned the magic of click and treat, choose a behavior you want to mark with the clicker. Let's say you want your dog to learn to lick his lips on cue. Watch your dog; click *the instant he licks his lips*. Timing is *everything* with a clicker. If you click a fraction of a second after he finishes licking his lips, you'll be rewarding something else—like having his tongue in his mouth!

🐕 Every time he licks his lips, click, say "yummy!" and then give him a reward. After a surprisingly small number of times of catching your dog doing something right, you'll see the lightbulb go on: "I get the magic click when I lick my lips!" He'll begin to offer the behavior. When he does, click and say "yummy!" and let him know that you're very happy he was so brilliant that he figured out the World's Greatest Trick!

🐕 Now that your dog has begun to understand that you want him to lick his lips, see if he has linked it with your cue—the word "yummy." Look at him and say "yummy!" The odds are he'll respond by licking his lips. Now you have a trick! You can say, "Was my cooking absolutely *yummy*?" And he'll respond by licking his lips. Pretty cool!

3. Shaping a behavior using a clicker.

🐕 More complicated tricks require *shaping*. For example, you might want to teach your dog to wave, but he doesn't offer this behavior naturally. It's easy to shape a behavior—you just click the closest thing your dog does to the behavior, and then click again when he comes closer.

🐕 In the example of teaching a dog to wave, you'd click and reward when the dog lifts his paw. Soon he'll be lifting his paw and looking expectantly for the click and reward. After he's done it a few times, *don't* click when he just picks up his paw a little. Almost every time, the dog will look at you and hold his paw up a little higher, almost shouting, *"Don't you see me??!! I've lifted my paw for you!"* As soon as he raises his paw that extra amount, click and treat. Over the course of several sessions, continue to ask for slightly more, and soon he'll be holding his paw up high and waving. Once he's done that, name the behavior– so as he waves, you click and treat and say "howdy!" Once you've shaped the behavior and named it, it's a trick that you can ask for on cue. Turn to your dog and say, "howdy!" and he'll wave!

Using Lure and Reward or Modeling Techniques

Although clickers are a great tool for positive training, they aren't the only fun and happy way to teach your dog. I don't use a clicker when I train my dogs. Some behaviors are easier to teach with *lure and reward* or *modeling* techniques. Also, some people find that holding the clicker gets too confusing and complicated. Here are some examples using these two positive techniques:

1. **Lure and reward.** As you've probably guessed, with this technique the trainer lures a dog into the desired position and then rewards the dog.

    Let's say you want to teach your dog to spin. You might have to wait years for your dog to offer this behavior so you can click and reward it. Instead, with the lure and reward method, you'll hold a treat in front of the dog's nose, say "spin" and lead the dog in a tight circle with the delicious treat. When he completes the circle, give him the reward saying, "good spin!" Soon you can take the food out of your hand and just hold your fingers in front of the dog's nose, saying "spin" and leading him into the spin. Over time, use your hands less and less to lure him into place—soon he'll just be responding to your command of "spin!"

2. **Modeling.** Sometimes it's easiest for both of you to just show your dog what you want by *gently* and *happily* holding him in the position you want him to be. That's called modeling.

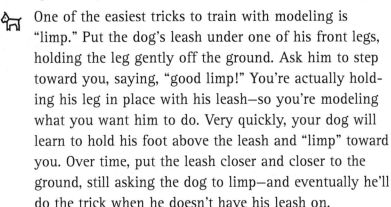 One of the easiest tricks to train with modeling is "limp." Put the dog's leash under one of his front legs, holding the leg gently off the ground. Ask him to step toward you, saying, "good limp!" You're actually holding his leg in place with his leash—so you're modeling what you want him to do. Very quickly, your dog will learn to hold his foot above the leash and "limp" toward you. Over time, put the leash closer and closer to the ground, still asking the dog to limp—and eventually he'll do the trick when he doesn't have his leash on.

Adding a Hand Signal

It's always snazzy to have a dog do a trick on a hand signal. And if you're subtle, the humans in the room might not even notice the signal. That's part of the magic of your tricky dog!

Here's how to teach using a hand signal:

If you're teaching a trick using the lure and reward method, your hand movements to lure the dog into place become the hand signal. For example, when you taught your dog to spin, you held your hand in front of his nose and lured him into a circle. Your hand signal for "spin" might be a circular motion above the dog's head, reminding him of the way he was taught to spin.

You can add a hand signal to any trick a dog knows. For example, if you've taught your dog to speak on command, you can later point to him every time you ask him to speak. He'll quickly learn to speak when you point, just as reliably as he does the trick when you say "speak." It's fun having a dog who speaks on a hand signal. For example, you can be singing and turn and point to your dog to do the back-up doo-wops. Or you can ask him the square root of nine and keep pointing until he barks three times.

Tricks are fun for both you and your dog, and are a marvelous way to bond. They're usually easy to teach and you're only limited by your imagination!

Suggested Reading

Dog Tricks for Dummies by Sarah Hodgson, Wiley Publishing, $19.95

Clicker Fun: Dog Tricks and Games Using Positive Reinforcement by Deborah Jones, Howln Moon Press, $19.95

Dog Tricks by Captain Arthur J. Haggerty and Carol Lea Benjamin, Black Dog & Leventhal, $14.98